Dial Me Naked

Dial Me Naked

Maria DeStefano

Writers Club Press
San Jose New York Lincoln Shanghai

Dial Me Naked

Writers Club Press
an imprint of iUniverse, Inc.

For information address:
iUniverse, Inc.
5220 S. 16th St., Suite 200
Lincoln, NE 68512
www.iuniverse.com

Adult content

ISBN: 0-595-24420-3

Printed in the United States of America

FORWARD

On a warm August day in 2001, I decided to ask myself some questions. "Why have I been involved in the adult industry for nearly seven years? Why did I ever start a phone sex line?" More importantly, "What purpose does this all have?"

I have a constant need to be accomplishing something, learning and/or passing it on to others. It was frightening to think that the last seven years were of no value except to pay the bills. There had to be more. I sat at my desk, looking at a blank computer monitor when I heard a little voice in my head. (I didn't literally hear one!) It said, "Write about it dummy. Tell people what you've learned." Yeah, that's it, but a book about stripping and phone sex? What good would that do other than entertain? I didn't question my intuition and began writing.

Then, on September 11, 2001, our world changed.

All the serious books that I have in my head would have to wait. Maybe we all need some entertainment now. Some light hearted reading to have fun with and still learn something about others who share our world. I've amused myself by writing this. Hope it does the same for you!

CONTENTS

Forward v

Part One—Take It All Off 1

A Funny Story—Bathroom talk 3

Lorie's Story 8

More Little Inconveniences 12

More Things Generally Not Known: 16

$$$ The Money $$$ Club Cash 18

Gifts and Offers 25

The Customers: Some Nice—Some, Not So Nice 33

The Girls: 48

The Private World: Private One on One Dancing 71

Bachelor Parties/Stags: 82

Part Two—Talk Dirty To Me **107**

Q's & A's 108

The Phone Calls 112

The "Normal" Calls: *113*

Be My Neighbor: *119*

The Older Woman: *121*

The Younger Woman *124*

Voyeurism *128*

Public Places *133*

Fetishes and Fantasies 141

Feet & Shoes *141*

Panty Fetishes *145*

Little Penis *152*

Naughty Boy! *156*

Really Different Fetishes—Some Nasty Ones: *163*
Wierdos *177*
Cross Dress Me *184*
Bad Girls *191*
Yes Mistress—No Mistress: *192*
Public Humiliation: *202*
Conclusion 205
About The Author: 207
Book Description 209

Part One

Take It All Off

Have you ever wondered what really goes on in a strip bar, at a bachelor party or in the private dance rooms? What is being talked about in the dressing rooms and bathrooms? Or....how about the lady who operates the phone sex line? What is she doing while she's talking to clients and what does she honestly look like? Well, I wondered about all that too and had to find out the hard way, by doing it all myself and now I can tell you first hand. So let's have some fun! Please enjoy being entertained by my true stories and information and of course, happy reading!

I'm going to tell you what goes into being an exotic dancer, stripper, topless dancer, or whatever name you'd care to use. We'll explore what it's like to be in those crowded bars and dance naked in front of men and women you don't know. We'll see how much fun this business can be as well as the down sides of it all. I'll take you on memorable bachelor parties with me and let you know how those guys truly behave when they get completely smashed and naked women are put in front of them. What is it like to dance privately in some stranger's home with a bodyguard posted outside? I'll tell you about some scary incidents where things got danger-ous as well as some very amusing stories that will keep you laughing.

Then there's the phone sex. I'll let you in on some really interesting fantasies and some very odd and strange fetishes. Even being a writer, I couldn't come up with some of these on my own! Many questions and curiosities will be answered. How do I feel personally about the guys I talk to? Do women call? Are couples ever interested? What's it like to be on the Internet where strangers know intimate details about your life? Is there any danger in it? Are there ever obsessive fans or worse yet, stalkers? Oh…you're in for some interesting reading. Let's start with a funny story that includes a female friend, her husband and myself, at a local strip bar

A Funny Story—Bathroom talk

A funny thing happened on the way to the ladies room. I was socializing at a local strip bar, the first one I ever visited as well as the first I worked at. This was also the initial bar I eventually danced at.

It didn't seem like four years had passed since the opening of the bar. I felt completely comfortable sitting in the large padded chairs, talking to dancers and chatting with customers. It was certainly a lot different than opening night when I got my first look at seven or eight beautiful women strip off their long evening gowns in front of people they'd never seen before. Even when every stitch was off, all seemed to be quite fine and comfortable. It was sure "interesting" serving drinks to men, just inches away from seven or eight bare bottoms.

We had to wear a sexy uniform consisting of a tuxedo type halter with tails, a bow tie, skimpy panty bottom and tights, along with heels. It was also the first place that I ultimately got the nerve to take off the waitress uniform and become a dancer myself. This is a small club where everyone has a good time, the atmosphere ordinarily laid back and customers as well as entertainers enjoy themselves. In general, the girls seem to work well together and have fun, even though the job was, and still is, literally back breaking.

It was a Thursday night, if I remember correctly and a female friend and I were treating her husband to a birthday evening, where the lucky birthday boy didn't have to spend a dime. We brought him to the bar, where he delighted in viewing all the pretty ladies. One girl in particular had a great attitude and the looks to match, so we soon employed her to indulge our guest in a private table dance. In this bar, a table dance means that the dancer takes the client over to a somewhat secluded area where she dances for him alone. There is no contact allowed between the dancer and the customer, as it is a completely nude bar where alcohol is served. In a more private setting, she can give him her full attention. *Rules and regulation vary from state to state and even from town to town.*

While the birthday boy was enjoying his dance, a friend and myself retrieved balloons and a big cake from the car, carefully bringing them into the bar. We put fifty-two candles on it and upon returning from his dance, we surprised him with everything, including everyone singing "Happy Birthday." Needless to say, he was quite elated and shared his cake with anyone who wanted some. Since names have been changed, we shall call our guest of honor Robert.

In the meantime, my friend Jill, Robert's wife, had to use the rest room. She was recuperating from a broken leg and having a difficult time moving about on crutches, but nature called. Here's where it gets funny. I escorted her to the bathroom and held the door open. She wasn't having an easy time hobbling into this tiny rest room. There was a sink on one end, a full sized mirror on the opposite wall and a tiny stall for the toilet. The whole room was the size of a closet. I was surprised that Jill didn't fall and break the other leg, with all the clothing and tote bags strewn about the floor and sink. This was not intended to be a dressing room, although some ladies preferred not to go down a flight of stairs into the basement to the actual dressing room. Although beautiful, large and well lit, going up and down stairs on those high heels gets tiring, so, some girls just kept their things in the little bathroom upstairs.

Anyway, back to the story…Upon opening the door for Jill, we saw a dancer bent over, looking like a piece of folded bread, just a couple of inches away from the full length mirror. Her very long, silky blond hair was draping across the floor. One had to be careful not to step on it. Her bare rear end was facing the mirror and in this sandwich like position that she appeared to be looking intently at something. She was. Her crotch to be exact. She got up, adjusted her lacy white G-string, smiled, and left the ladies room.

Jill just watched silently, but the look on her face was priceless. I remember a time when I had the same puzzled look so it was rather funny to me. Jill didn't even have to ask. I just looked at her and said, "She was checking for the string." "Huh?" was Jill's only response. "The string. You know, the string for the tampon," I answered. "Oh…that string! You know. I was wondering about that. What do the girls do when it's their time of month?" "Well, it's simple," I replied. "You take the string, cut it, wrap it and then shove it, as far up as you can. Then check to make sure it doesn't show." "Oh!" said Jill, "I guess I'm getting an education of sorts."

With that comment, Heather, the pretty, curvy blond entered the ladies room again, once more looking in the mirror and wiping herself with baby wipes. *No, she doesn't have a fetish with her crotch.* She was a little annoyed with her new pair of delicate, white G-string panties and matching top. She remarked that while table dancing for Jill's husband, she noticed that lint from the brand new undies was sticking to her body. This club, like many, has a lot of ultra violet lighting, which will show every bit of lint, no matter where it is. It especially likes to cling to body hair, and what little Heather had, attracted the lint, which looked very bright under the lights. Despite this drawback, those ultraviolet lights sure make all sorts of flaws vanish. I made a comment to Heather about how Jill was enjoying her new education…and then the stories started.

Here's a little warning. Some of these stories, now very funny to me were really "gross" at the time I heard them, so take this with a grain of salt. There are lots of "nicer" stories, but the gross ones make for great bathroom gossip. I said I'd tell the truth, so here it is.

Heather said, "Hey, were you here the time that a girl on stage pulled her panties to the side to flash a customer, and accidentally grabbed her tampon string at the same time?" Jill was turning a nice shade of pale green when she heard this. Heather continued. "She just yanked the tampon right out and stood there giggling." Jill's mouth was open now.

Heather told us that the girl on stage said to the audience, "Oh look, my tampon fell out!" Thankfully, I wasn't there for that one. I'm not sure what I'd have done if it had been to me. Try not to be completely humiliated and make a joke of it? Apologize and politely get off the stage? Run as fast as possible to the ladies room? Faint? Throw up? Never return to the club or dancing again? All of the above? I'm sure I wouldn't have thought it was funny like that girl did. I doubt that the guys at the stage though it was funny, do you?

Now, if you were a woman reading this, what would you have done? So you may not be a stripper, but let's say you were trying to be sexy for your significant other and that happened to you? Never mind…let's not think about it.

Here's another story. I call this the all time, really nasty "poop story." A male friend and a buddy of his were there and related it first hand. This incident took place at another bar, where the stage is about chest level to the customers sitting down. There's a lower "shelf" a few inches down for their drinks. When the dancer comes around and literally gets on the floor in front of them, the view is quite good and they see everything pretty close up.

Here's what happened. The money went up, the girl came by, danced a bit, and then bent down to a squatting position, naked. Unfortunately, when she squatted, she lost control of her bodily functions and "splat!" She pooped all over the stage. *Hey, I told you this one was nasty.*

If that wasn't bad enough, my friend's buddy has a twisted sense of humor and thought it was the funniest thing he'd ever seen. He went into such a fit of laughter that his chair fell completely back to the floor with him still in it. Picture a chubby, cherub faced, buzzed cut blond with pudgy cheeks and glasses, on his back with his feet in the air, laughing out of control. OK, maybe you don't want to picture that, but it must have been a sight. The poor girl ran off the stage, into the dressing room and immediately out of the bar, never to return. *Can't blame her, can you?* The hysterical customer was asked to leave. The worst thing is that no one wanted to clean the stage. All the big, tough bouncers wouldn't go near it. Eventually another dancer came out and cleaned it up.

So, this is the stuff Heather and I subjected Jill to that night in the bar. For a somewhat prissy schoolteacher type, she seemed to handle it well and to my knowledge, still continues to visit the bars with her hubby.

If you thought this story was interesting, keep going, because there are plenty more. The funny ones, the good ones, the bad ones and the ones that you just can't believe are true, but they are, believe me.

First, I'd like to take you to different places and share some experiences with you. We'll go from the little bars to the classiest clubs. Here goes:

Lorie's Story

It's a typical Friday night at a local downtown strip bar. Not one of the fancy places with extravagant lighting or a glamorous stage....no....just a regular hangout where many of the same guys come each weekend to have a few drinks, relax and watch their favorite ladies. This business has a good turnover so there's always a new face or two added. The atmosphere is pretty much the same all the time. Music is playing, bordering on the loud side, ranging from the DJ's selection to a variety of dance and rock with an occasional blues tune thrown in. The bartenders are running back and forth to keep up with the needs of the patrons. The focus for those seated at the bar is, of course, not the music or the beer, but on the women, who in this particular bar, are allowed to dance fully nude even while alcohol is being served.

This Friday evening brings something a little different to the already party atmosphere. A tall brunette stands at the front of the stage. She's on stage near the main entrance and greets the eyes of every person, male or female that enter the bar. The slender brunette dances around erotically wearing a hot red bra and matching thong panty, satin and sexy. Trimmed with a black leather cap on her head, she wears a choker with a series of chains attached and is carrying a small whip, giving the sexy satin look a rough edge. She's wearing red stilettos that show off her painted toenails. Her long fingernails match and her gold chain waist belt moves as she does. Her dark hair is long, thick and wavy and her eyes are bedroom brown.

The stage connects to the bar at several points, allowing her to entertain directly in front of a customer. As she spots money up on the bar and moves from place to place, she is careful not to bump into anyone's drink with her high heels. This task becomes even more difficult as she kneels down on the simple black bar to get closer to the gentleman now directly in front of her, getting as close as six inches from him. Believe it or not, in many areas of this place, the bar IS the stage. There is no shelf just below the area where the girl dances for the customer to put a drink or ashtray as in other bars. It's just a bar, which she must share with the customer in a very close area.

Picture yourself trying to move around in five-inch heels in a confined space, above the ground, dancing up and down for dollars, sitting your bottom where hands, ashtrays, drinks, and other bottoms have been. Sound glamorous now? Lorie is five foot nine inches tall in bare feet, which makes her over six feet on stage. Although it's difficult for her not to knock someone's drink over or hit someone in the face with those heels, the gentlemen here sure love her long legs. She is also skilled in her movements, which is the main reason that no customer has received a black eye.

Tonight is her birthday. She calls herself Lorie, which may or may not be her real name. One would have to guess, as it's not a "plastic" name. You know…Starlight, Sunshine, Emerald, etc. Lorie is a nice "normal" name, which seems to fit her even it it's not the real thing. As she parades around in her fiery red outfit for her half-hour set, a friend and co-worker who calls herself "Ash," is seen bringing in a cake with the seven dwarfs adorning the top. Two big candles both with the number two are placed side by side for the number twenty-two. Lorie is more than thrilled. She tells everyone how special she feels. Someone or maybe a few people thought of her tonight and remembered this day.

Lorie is so happy. She's off the stage now and sharing her cake with choice friends in the bar. She's been drinking some and is getting a little silly. Well, it's her birthday. *Not that drinking is something unknown in a strip bar.* It is safe to say Lorie felt important and cared about, which is something that's not easy to come by in this industry. Basically, you are only what you look like. Sad, as there is a real human side to dancers, which few see, or want to see.

It's almost 1:30 am now and nearly time to wrap things up. Lorie, like everyone else is tired, although by this time the few drinks have turned into a few more. Everyone else is tired also. They may not show it on their faces, but their red knees give it away. After all, they all work seven, one half-hour sets. This club requires one half hour on the stage, and one half-hour off, most of the stage work being done on their knees. It's 2:00 am now and as the music goes off the lights come on. Lingering customers are being nudged out and the girls are leaving, some getting rides, others being walked to their cars by a bouncer. Tonight was relatively calm with a happy atmosphere and the birthday theme going on. There were no fights and no attention was paid to the usual "less than legal" things that go on in this and every other place. More about that later. For now, the place gets locked up and the night continues. It's another day

Lorie's story goes on a little more. On another Tuesday at 7:00 PM, she arrives and is getting ready for her first set of the evening. Wearing a shiny black miniskirt that is below her navel, it's short enough to see her black lace G-string. Her top is a teeny, black, see-through halter to match the skirt, revealing her breasts. She takes her place on stage but after only fifteen minutes she gets down and goes back to the dressing room. She sits, crying on a step near the floor, completely breaking down. Why? Did she get hurt? Did someone say something to her? Did an old boyfriend come in with another woman? What? Nothing like that. Lorie just can't do this anymore. Well she can't do it without alcohol or drugs anyway. Lots of alcohol or drugs. She needs it just to work.

She has two sons who live with their father because she can't care for them. Although she visits them, she knows she can't be the mother they need at this time. So she makes a major decision to join the military and straighten herself up. Her new problem is that she needs to take a drug test. She's had no drugs for three weeks and realizes she's come to a crossroads. She can stop dancing now and will have no money to live on as she has months to go before she actually goes to boot camp. Or, go back to drugs so she can work until it's time to go. Either way, it's a no win situation for her.

This is the type of lady who should never have become a dancer. It's a stressful profession for anyone with the most together head, but for her it's just too much. The best way I can relate to Lorie's situation is to imagine myself working in a store full of chocolate and being told that I shouldn't have any or I'll get sick. I don't think I'd be able to handle the temptation. Same thing for those people who use alcohol and drugs just to be able to get through their day. In this industry, it's everywhere and many times it's free.

I eventually lost track of Lorie, but I hope to someday run into her and find her healthy, happy and reunited with her beautiful boys. In all honesty, I don't think that will be the case, at least not for a very long time.

This is just one small story to fill you in on the up side and the down side, all at one time. A future chapter will be devoted only to stories, but for now, a taste of everything.

Let's get back to the daily life of a dancer…

MORE LITTLE INCONVENIENCES

Stripping and tripping sometimes go hand in hand. Most dancers, including myself have moved fluidly on to the stage, full of confidence and poise, smiling seductively, only to trip up the last step. This takes all that confidence and squashes it quickly, believe me. It's not easy to try and keep a "dignified" look at that point. What can you do? Gotta continue or maybe lose your job. Another fun stunt is to make it on to the stage just fine, only to trip right smack in the middle of everything. *Not like I've done that or anything.* There are some possible reasons for this one.

1. Someone spilled something on the stage floor like water or a drink.
2. One of the other girls was wearing oils to make her skin glisten and it left a residue on the stage, which annoys everyone else.
3. One can trip over a long gown.
4. Some of us are just plain clumsy.
5. Here is one of my repeated mishaps. I fell off my platforms! That one isn't just embarrassing, it hurts too!

There's one bar in the downtown area where I now live that has "breaks" in it. There's about a four-foot space where the stage breaks for the bartenders to walk back and forth. That's nice for the bartenders, but what about the girls? Well, there are railings and they have to grab on and literally jump across. Oh, it's fun, believe me. I've tried it. Have a couple of drinks, which is allowed on the job at most places, and try it. You end up at times dangling by your arms trying to get back up, or just land on the floor and climb up again. It doesn't help girls who are just over five feet tall, like myself. Jumping back up is NOT an option. Wait till you hear what the bar itself is like that the girls must dance on. You won't believe it. More about that later.

Now bear with me, whether a lady or a gentleman reading this, I really feel it's important to know what goes into being a dancer before we get into the more interesting material. Ladies, you might want to think twice before you take this on as a profession and gentlemen, you'll appreciate what the women go through. Just try it for a night! This next section will put you in the right frame of mind to move on.

Let's see…. Here's a question for you ladies. Have you ever felt like not shaving your legs for a while, even a day or two? This is not the case for an exotic dancer. Although the costumes and makeup are fun and glamorous, there's that all too familiar razor burn. I'll explain. Even you guys know what razor burn is. Well, imagine it all over your legs and also some very delicate places. Try shaving your private areas every day and see if you can escape an uncomfortable, bumpy burn.

It appears that the strip bar etiquette of the 90's and into the millennium is to shave one's private area in some form or another. Some shave completely, others leave a little and some prefer shapes such as hearts. I saw an arrow once…*Just thought I'd throw that in.* Whatever you choose, your skin and a razor generally meet at very frequent intervals. This is not so bad if you have naturally light hair as you can get away with shaving less. Now try having naturally black hair like I do. Oh. That's fun. Five o'clock shadow rings a bell. When working a double shift, I actually had to shave twice in one day! This is not unlike a guy with dark hair who has to attend a function after a long day at the office. I do sympathize with those men!

The thing is…when you do this night after night it really gets to be uncomfortable, sometimes producing little red bumps that itch, burn and look terrible. Make up irritates it more, but you have to use some or it will show on stage. What's the best solution? A quick fix is roll on deodorant. Yup, it works. Or, you can take a day or two off which is not a good idea if you're already scheduled, or don't try to work five days in a row. It may seem minor, but it's a real pain in the rear…which brings me to another thing.…

"Stage Rash," or "stage butt" as I call it. At some clubs, floor work is allowed. This is where a girl is allowed to literally get on the floor in front of the client and perform. I'll go into details of the dancing later, but let's just say for now that she can get into whatever position she wants. In some places, a thong or G-string is required, but in others, like where I live, it's fully, and I mean….show all…nude. Anyhow, from putting one's fanny repeatedly on the stage where everyone's shoes have been, one can get little red bumps on one's tush. It can itch, but usually doesn't. It just looks awful. Generally, if a shower is taken right after work it will go away the next day, depending on how sensitive one's skin is. Even as olive skinned as I am and do not have sensitive skin, I've had to skip a day or two because of an unsightly rash. The solution? Take a towel or little decorative rug around if you must get on the floor to sit on, or just get on your knees and don't let your fanny touch the stage if possible. Like I said before….what a pain in the butt.

A Tan Rule?

Here's a good one. It isn't unusual for a club to have written rules posted in the dressing room. Some more common rules include arrangements for smoking cigarettes, bring your own liquor, time schedules, late fines and things of that sort. Another rule that is usually posted is one about the proper attire. In some places a dancer must have her rear end and/or breasts covered when she leaves the stage. I can understand all of these things being important, but a tan rule? This is what was posted on the wall in one club I worked at: "All dancers must maintain proper weight and a proper tan." Give me a break. This is New England! We can only tan a few months out of the entire year! Oh yes, there are those tanning booths to help things along if it's not July. I have nothing against them, but on a regular basis, they do help to speed up the aging process along a little faster than one would like.

This ridiculous rule wasn't too bad for me, being darker skinned, but those poor kids who are light. They had to subject themselves to tanning all the time. Fortunately, there are great self-tanning creams on the market, and I've also noticed that in many places it's becoming acceptable to have a more natural look..

The biggest inconvenience about being a dancer has to be that darn monthly thing. It's not easy being a nude or topless dancer and going through this every month. We've covered earlier what must be done about the tampon and string, but there's always the concern about "when" it's going to start. For any men reading this, you need to know that a woman's period usually gives no warning. It just starts. Fortunately, and most often, it doesn't start with a vengeance and we have time to deal with it. All that aside, there's the constant worry about staining costumes and undies, especially on stage, or during a private or lap dance. Some ladies with heavy periods just have to stay out of work for at least the first day. That's number one on the inconvenience list.

More Things Generally Not Known:

Many people assume that a dancer is given a huge shift pay just to go to work. WRONG. Most clubs either charge the dancer just to work there or in places where they don't charge, the girls work on tips alone. Years ago there were shift pays in some of the smaller clubs, but not very often now.

In some clubs, the dancer must tip out the club. One very small club had a $20 tip out per night. Girls didn't even get a free drink or a discount and on a quiet Monday or Tuesday night, it wasn't easy to make money. Yet, everyone paid.

On a larger scale, there are clubs where it's $30 and up to walk in the door to work, plus numerous tip-outs. It starts with the valet parking, which is optional. Keep in mind that most of these valets are young, good looking guys, maybe eighteen to twenty-one years old. They treat the girls like gold and are so cute that you just can't help but let them park for you and tip them. Next there's the DJ. The girl can usually request music she likes when she's on stage and a tip out is required.

In the large clubs there are women in the dressing rooms who help the dancers. There can be hair stylists and make up artists who provide services to anyone who would like them. These ladies need to be tipped. I've seen bathroom attendants who just sit there and hand out towels as well as keep the bathroom clean with a tip jar in plain sight. Many clubs have a "house mother" who tends to the needs of the dancers. This is one of those jobs that vary widely in different places, but it's not an easy one no matter where it is. Sometimes a housemother is only responsible for making sure the girls are on stage at the proper time as well as taking care of scheduling and keeping the peace. Sound easy? Not really. A club can book ten to hundreds of dancers in a night, only to have a much smaller amount show up. I danced at a small place where only four to six girls were on during the afternoon and more than once there were only two of us until they got someone else in. This is not a lot of fun for the customer or us.

There are other "house mothers" who tend to many different things. I've seen places where she has a cabinet full of things, like tampons, sewing needs, bandages, ointments, aspirin, antacids and nail glue, (very important), among other things. She will sew something on a costume or pin a strap for a "quick fix" and get the girls what they might need.

At some places there are women hired specifically to care for costumes. Along with fixing and mending, she will hang clothing, steam, iron, sew and anything else pertaining to costume care. In some smaller clubs one of the dancers is hired to double as a housemother. This job is generally given to a more responsible, older dancer. *Understand that in this business, thirty IS older!* Along with her regular job of dancing, she'll receive shift pay each week. Sometimes she is tipped and sometimes not.

You see how expensive these large clubs can be, just to work at? Of course, the money there is great so it does balance out. As for the other employees, let me tell you…the costume lady, DJ, bartender, etc., do pretty well also. Figure anywhere from 50 to 100 ladies, and more in places, all giving a tip of $5, $10 or more. Not a bad take for one night, even in s smaller club with 10 to 20 ladies. So, with all these club expenses on the part of the dancer, not to mention costume costs, how does she make any money? There are plenty of options.

$$$ The Money $$$
Club Cash

The main reason anyone becomes a dancer is pretty obvious. MONEY. There is plenty to be made depending on the club and what you want to do. There is stage work, table dancing and lap dancing, plus VIP rooms.

Stage Work: Dancing on a platform or a stage where the customers sit around watching the lady perform. Ordinarily fifteen minutes or so if she's alone, more if she's working with other ladies at the same time. In most cases, the stage is a "showcase" of sorts where the gentlemen decide on their lady of choice for private dances later. *That's the idea, anyway.*

If the place is crowded and the girl is working the stage, she can quickly go from customer to customer, giving them a little dance and move on to the next. Try it if you think it's easy…many times it's dancing for dollars, literally, but it can pay off later. If it's a quiet shift, there's often one guy in the small crowd who fancies the girl on stage, giving her money over and over. It's sort of his way to keep her dancing for him. She'll pay close attention to him and bring him straight into the table dance area or the VIP room after she's finished on stage. It could be as little as one dance, or many.

When the gentleman is spending money on more than a couple of dances and drinks and visits frequently, there's a good possibility he'll become a "regular," visiting the club specifically to see that particular girl. This is what all dancers strive for, the regular customers. Those guys who know your schedule and will only come in for you. They feel special, they feel comfortable, they feel they're on a personal level with the dancer. They spend.

Table Dances: These are commonly done right at the table, in full view of everyone else. A "not so private" dance, but still just for one. The dancer pays attention only to the gentleman she's in front of, dancing as close to him as the club allows. Sometimes she's as much as three feet away or as little as a few inches. Contact with the customer is allowed in places. Table dances can cost as little as $5 to $10 per dance. *I haven't seen a five-dollar table dance for almost ten years.*

Lap Dances: Same as table dances, except she's on your lap! Most of what I've seen involves the dancer bumping and grinding the gentleman as much or as little as she wants, as well as dancing for him. Most places insist that the dancer wear a bottom, although I have seen otherwise. Again, in most cases, the man must keep his hands to himself, with the dancer being able to touch him only. He can't. Commonly, lap dances start at $20 and go up, though I have seen $10 lap dances.

Vip Rooms: The VIP Rooms vary as much as the clubs. Some are just petitioned off areas, while others are much more private. Here are some examples:

One club, on the smaller side, has a big room with separate areas. There are plush chairs and a table where the dancer and customer can sit, talk and drink. When it comes time to dance though, the little stage is behind a thick velvet rope with two poles on each side with definite distance kept between dancer and customer. The room itself has a glass front and a bouncer can see in at all times. Dances are $20 each. (Completely nude)

Another club, small but nice, has a back room with a small stage that's used on weekends only. The private areas consist of comfy armchairs for the customer and a small chair for the dancer. There are oriental screens that partition off the area, leaving a space so that it's not completely private. This is for the protection of the dancer as well as to make sure no "funny business" goes on. Dances are $20 each. (Completely nude)

Another place had "booths" with a platform for the dancer. The customer was completely hidden but when the dancer stood on the platform she was visible. The club was closed in the mid 90's and at that times, dances were $10 each. (Completely nude)

A very small club had a small back room with chairs lined up around the walls. There wasn't a whole lot of privacy, but it was a lap dance club and the guys were too busy enjoying themselves to care. In 2001, dances were only $10 each. The low price could be due to the girls wearing pasties and a G-string, plus a bottom, so there wasn't as much nudity as in other places.

A very large club had a beautiful back room with chairs, tables it's own doorman and waitress. This place was very exclusive, very classy and very expensive. The cost in 2001 was $100 for three dances, plus a two drink minimum with each drink being over $10, even for a soda. Dances on the floor at your table were $20 each. (Topless only) This club has a champagne atmosphere and the girls are all exquisite.

Panty & Lingerie Sales: Yes that's right. It's not something done all the time, but there are plenty of men who are struck by a girl that they realistically know won't be going home with him. Maybe he can take a "piece" of her home anyway, in the form of what she is wearing. Most of the time they will ask to take her panties home. I've not known many ladies that will just give them away …after all they are expensive. I personally have had men "buy" my undies, stockings, teddies and even costume jewelry. One man would bring in panty hose for the girl to dance in, pay for the dance, and then buy back the panty hose worn. Ooooh….that's a good story. I'll tell you about it later. I've also seen panty and T-shirt dances where all the dancers come out at once, wearing the items for sale. They are sold, along with a dance.

Pay For Conversation: There are times, especially after a private dance, where a client is fascinated with the lady who's entertaining him. If she'd like, she can sit, have a drink and talk to him. Usually these clients will become "regulars" and come back to see the same lady again. If there's a lot of money to be made that night, she can let the client know that her time is valuable and while she's enjoying their conversation, she could be out there entertaining other gentlemen. There are plenty of times that I've seen girls just sit, talk and party. That's fine but there isn't going to be any money unless she says something. Many times the gentleman will hand out a $20 bill just to have you sit and talk a while longer. I've known girls who were handed hundreds for the same thing. Depends on when, where and how much the guy can and wants to spend. If this isn't appealing to the customer, he'll simply see you on stage again next set. Either way, the name of the game is money. After all, this is a job. So, let's get into what it's like on a daily basis….

The Routine

For many people outside the adult entertainment industry, the job looks easy, glamorous and seems like one big party. At times IT IS one big party, at others, just the opposite.

On a typical night, or day, the dancer carries her costumes to and from work. Some have their gowns neatly placed on hangers with plastic covering while others just throw everything in a big bag and go. On the whole, I've seen more disorganized costume bags than organized. It's hard to keep it neat when there's so much to bring. Again, keep in mind we're talking about clubs where middle America goes. Places where regular guys who work hard for their money visit. A club where a guy can go in with as little as $30 and still have a measure of fun, though limited. Cover charge, one drink, tip for the waitress, and still a few bucks left over for the stage although, $30 is NOT recommended.

Anyway, in come the ladies, lugging their bags full of costumes, make up, jewelry, sometimes wigs, and in some places, they bring music. Since clubs and dressing rooms vary so much we'll stay focused on this smaller, relaxed, comfortable place like the first place I danced as I mentioned before. Well, the dressing room, which was just beautiful, was, unfortunately, behind the bar, through the kitchen and down in the basement of the club. Sounds awful, but except for the seemingly endless trek to get there, the room was quite nice. Built especially for the bar when it was sold and reopened, there was really no other place to put a dressing room up stairs.

So, drag your stuff in, down the stairs, grab a spot on the floor or a chair and settle in. Closet space provides hangers for nicer outfits and lockers are available.…you supply your own locks. Make up is put on the counters. I use the term "makeup" loosely. Of course there is the regular assortment of eye makeup, pencils, lip and cheek color along with face powder. Add to that, eyelashes, cover up for under eyes & face, plus body makeup for any bruise, blemish, rash, etc., deodorant, perfumes, lotions, hair spray, combs, brushes, feminine products and more. We were fortunate to have lots of mirrors, counter space and great lighting. Wait till you hear about some of the dressing rooms.…I'll bet your shed looks better.

Time to transform. Some ladies do a total makeover. From a jeans and tee, no make up look to glitz and glamour, including excessive makeup, stand out lips, teased, curled or wild hair. Others prefer a more natural look, with simple hair, embellishing on their own natural beauty.

Costumes differ from place to place. The larger clubs require certain attire, such as evening gowns or short cocktail dresses only. In the more relaxed places, anything goes. Lingerie is always a winner. Silk, satin, lace, pretty bra and panty sets, teddies, etc. are popular with the gentlemen. Long gowns with slits that say "just peek," paired with garters and stockings, seem to please many a viewer. The short, sexy dresses are great for "bending over" and are such a tease. Personally, I always wore stockings or thigh highs with an occasional garter belt. The stage floor can do a number on the legs and I found it a protection as well as very provocative. This is especially true when you're working in a club where floor work is allowed.

There are always regular costumes. Some have sequins and beads and others have themes. It's fun to have a different look and use your music to match it. Here are some things I've done and could work for you ladies at home too:

All White: I've even gone as far as carrying little flowers for the customers. Use music like Madonna's "Like a Virgin," or Billy Idol's "White Wedding." It's fun to look so innocent and be so seductive. Wouldn't this be fun to do as a surprise anniversary gift?

Dress like a teacher:…Hand out pencils and paper to the guys and dance to "Hot for Teacher" by VanHalen! Surprise, or rather, shock your honey with this one, especially if teaching is your real profession!

Wear all red: Seductive music such as Enigma, or soundtracks like "Sliver" or "91/2 weeks" are a definite turn on. On Valentine's Day, give out red heart stickers. The personal contact with the client when you put the sticker on is great. They love it. At home, strip out of the red outfit, leaving only a bow for him to untie. Then he can play with his present.

Denim:….Wear boots and a cowboy hat and dance to some movin' country music. I loved my ruffled Daisy Dukes and a bra type halter-top. Try leaving the boots on, only the boots. Your cowboy will love it.

All Black:…A definite favorite. Find the sexiest music possible and/or good old rock. I've used whips to "snap" the money off of the stage with some dark, seductive music…and more. Black works no matter what. At home, maybe your guy would like you to be more dominant and bolder than usual. Tell him what you want and make him do it till you're pleased.

The Schoolgirl: A desired theme of the customers. The typical plaid skirt with a short white blouse, exposing the midriff, knee socks and a ponytail. Fun to spice it up with a notebook, little purse and a lollipop. This would be great to do if your guy is the teacher in the family.

*Note: The little "extras" above are intended for personal dance at home, not for a club. When it's a job, sex of any kind isn't the idea—unless you're in a state where that is legal and under the rules and regulations of the state, county or town.

The Atmosphere

Bar shifts are often six to eight hours, but a girl can usually work more if she'd like. At some clubs I've worked at, we're talking about one-half hour sets, alternating on and off the stage. That means you dance for a half-hour, then are only off stage for a half-hour. In that time off, you're supposed to change, socialize, fix your makeup, do a table dance, and pee! That's why, many times the customer goes right from their chair to the table dance area! At some of the better clubs, a dancer would be on stage for about fifteen or twenty minutes and only every hour and a half. The rest of the time was spent on socializing and dancing privately. Great....if the club is crowded, not so great if it's quiet.

A party zone: The atmosphere in general really is a party zone. There's upbeat music on all the time, people are having a good time and alcohol is always flowing freely. Seriously, every time one would turn around, there'd be someone offering to buy a drink or one was in front of you. It's very easy to end your shift and take your tired feet right to the bar and relax for a while. From a financial standpoint, it's not always a bad idea either. The regular customers do appreciate a little extra time spent just on them after you're finished with a long shift.

At just about every bar I've encountered, there's always a bartender or bouncer to walk you to your car. This great little out of the way bar I've worked at had the bouncer stand outside until the ladies were in their cars with the doors locked and driving away. They'd even stay a minute or so extra to make sure no one was following, which isn't bad at all.

Gifts and Offers

I'd have to say that most of what you see in movies about eccentric men offering a dancer all sorts of gifts is most certainly true.

Just last year, I met a man who admittedly spent about $100,000 on a dancer over a period of time on everything from gifts to necessities to new and larger breasts. He also made a point to let everyone know that there was no sex of any kind involved. This was not a wealthy gentleman, but he was financially comfortable. Lonely after the passing of his wife, he found someone he was interested in. His reason for giving her so much for so little in return? He said he "liked her and wanted to help." Generous indeed but not usually what happens. Most guys do want something in return for that kind of generosity.

Love that lingerie: We ladies do love our lingerie, but sometimes left up to you men, we end up with a lot of very sexy items that are not always wearable. We do appreciate it though. One time during a late afternoon shift I danced for a nice business type gentleman. He had a big smile on his face; a fistful of dollars and even his eyes were smiling. Besides being very friendly, he'd had a few too many cocktails, which probably explains the smiling eyes. Anyhow…every time I'd leave to dance for someone else he'd put more money up, which meant I'd keep going back to him. He wore a sport coat, slacks and dress shoes. The top two buttons of his dress shirt were undone and I'd guess his tie was in the car. He had a light complexion, very blue eyes and blond hair. In his forties I found out later.

After my set, I went over to say thank you and he offered to buy me a drink. He ordered while I rushed back stage to change. I had very little time between sets as this bar scheduled everyone for that half-hour on/half hour off sets. Before I knew it, I was on stage once more, dancing for him again. His generosity on stage continued for three weeks and one day asked for my sizes and color preferences for lingerie. *I told him, of course!* The next week came in with all sorts of goodies. He was on a white theme I think, giving me a beautiful white satin bra and panty set with a matching satin appliquéd robe. A pink and white satin teddy, four pairs of thigh highs and four pair of lace panties in shades of pinks and lavender were also in the goodie bag. Add to that some very nice musk scented oil and good stage money. I was sure happy that day!

We later found out we had a lot in common with families and life circumstances and to this day still talk as friends and sometimes meet for lunch. Great guy.

More Undies: On my birthday, a gentleman brought me four bra and panty sets from Victoria Secret in deep green satin, soft peach lace, sexy red satin and a lavender lace. He even matched body lotions and candles. The next year he made me a professional birthday cake in the colors of my favorite football team along with three great books he knew I would like. Very sweet and genuine, I must say.

This gentleman as well as the previous one was simply being an admirer. They never asked for sex or anything like that and I know they didn't expect it either. Both were soft spoken, gentlemen who gave from the heart. Very refreshing.

I'll pay the mortgage: When I was still a waitress, I met a man who frequented the bar and spent a decent amount of money on table dances and drinks for the ladies. He'd usually pick one girl that he liked and pay for five or six dances. He was around the sixty-year mark, well dressed, often in a suit, very pleasant and always smiling. He was nice looking for a man of his years.

For a while he became infatuated with me and would tip me very well for drinks. At one time he knew I was going to have a birthday and asked what I'd like for a gift. I think he expected me to ask for clothing or jewelry. What I really wanted were tickets to a very good rock concert and I knew that he had connections. He came in the next week with four really good tickets and repeated the same gesture a few months later.....and all I did was waitress at that time! These aren't huge offers but remember this is a small club in a small city.

One day he asked me how much money I needed each week to pay my bills. I asked him why he wanted to know. He replied that he'd gladly pay what I asked if I'd "meet" with him once or twice a week for lunch and to relax. *Hmmm, wonder what "relax" meant.* Somehow I didn't think he meant watching TV or playing a board game. He was married and never said much about his wife, so I'm assuming it wasn't the happiest of marriages. It's a common story. There's money involved and sometimes people prefer to stay legally married to avoid financial complications. He wanted a mistress on the side. Who knows? Maybe his wife had someone also. I declined. To be perfectly honest, I simply wasn't attracted to him so even the possibility of a real date was out of the question. If he wasn't someone I could date, I didn't want to have just an "arrangement." Had he looked like our bartender at the time, I would have considered the possibility!

Take my 1967 classic: One afternoon, still at the same club, on a quiet, few customer day, I noticed a man at the end of the stage, with a group of dollar bills in front of him. I was on stage alone and of course went right over. He had striking black hair, thick and on the longish side, very big dark eyes and a darker olive complexion although he was Caucasian. He was on the quiet side, but friendly. After my time on stage was finished, he asked for a private dance. I believe I only danced two or three times for him. The club was not at all busy so I had time to sit and chat with him quite a bit. He explained that he was in there alone because he would come up to the area, from about 2 hours away, once a week to help a friend with work on his house. The friend was in a wheel chair and needed assistance.

Turns out that the gentleman with the black hair, who I'll call Vincent, had been injured and won a good sized settlement as well as benefits from his employer. He chose to volunteer some of his time to a less fortunate friend which I'm sure you'd agree was pretty nice. He would be in the area the next day and as I'd be working again, he said he'd bring lunch, which he did. When he left, he said he'd be up the following week when I was working and bring lunch again. He did. At this point he stopped asking for table dances. It was also at this point that I had to decide whether to keep things completely business or turn it personal. I chose the latter. Yes, you can meet nice guys at a strip bar. I accepted his phone number and after the poor guy gave me everything but his social security number, I gave him mine, phone number, not social security number, that is. For the record, I did tell him that I wanted a friendship only. *I now realize that guys just hate that "F" word.*

After talking for a few weeks I met him at a local mall, where he proceeded to buy me clothing, lingerie and things to wear on stage, as well lunch at a nice restaurant. We had a common ethnic background so we had plenty to talk about. I thought this would be a nice friendship. He wanted a girlfriend. We were on different trains, basically. It didn't click that way for me. *Guess I wanted everyone to look like our bartender!* I was honest about not wanting anything more than a friendship when his offers increased.

I must have seriously frustrated him because he offered me $1,000.00 to spend the night with him. Honestly, I wasn't holding out for that kind of offer. It just wasn't going to work.

Then came the car. This guy had a classic 1967 "something or other." It was a show car with all original parts and was worth a lot. The car was treated like a baby. He offered it to me if I'd be his girlfriend. I had an old car at the time. Just couldn't do it. I think that when you accept something or someone that you're really not into, the hassles and stress will outweigh the material rewards. Also, there were some serious issues that we clashed on. These things would never work in a relationship. I declined. I don't think my son, who was a young teen at the time wanted to talk to me for a while after that one. He loved that car.

Now if I'd have just kept it professional and inside the club, I probably would have ended up with lots of nice gifts, although not as good as a car. Instead I ended up in the long run with a friend who I still keep in contact with from time to time after six or seven years. I'd like to see him happy with someone special.

*Note: Keep in mind now, we're still talking about small clubs where I personally worked. This is just small scale. Things are a lot different in other places.

Let's take a trip: Vacations are probably one of the most common offers made to dancers. For one thing, if the guy is married, he can go someplace where no one knows him and relax freely. Also, they want an attractive woman on their arm and can basically pick and choose whom they'd like. Some want a blonde with large breasts; others want a tall, slender redhead. Some want a very young girl and still others want a more mature and believable woman such as myself, especially if the man is older.

One guy asked me to take a boat trip for a weekend. We'd be staying on the boat, but spend part of the time in New York City buying clothing and going to nightclubs. Shoes, purses and accessories would be included. Also a Broadway play. OK, this guy got my attention. He was a middle-aged man in his fifties, stout, with a tummy, and thinning gray hair with glasses. *I'm being polite*. You don't have to be a rocket scientist to know there had to be something more he wanted. I asked. He said he just wanted me to relax on the boat in a bikini during the day and keep him company. There's that "relax" word again. Then he added that it would be good if I had a girlfriend or two, as there would be two other gentlemen going. I just listened as he went on.

He went on to mention how "romantic" he was and how much he loved the stars, sunsets, sunrises, etc., but didn't like watching all of this alone. Then he threw in how much he likes to drink wine under the stars, sunset, sunrise, etc. and how it puts him in an amorous mood. Doesn't take too many brain cells to see where this was going. I believe I told him I'd be out of town that specific weekend. Yeah, I should have been totally honest, but oh well. So, there went a perfectly nice weekend in New York along with clothes and Broadway. He never called again. Doesn't matter. *He didn't even come close to the bartender!*

A $5,000.00 bracelet: These are gifts offered in clubs where there's more money to throw around. The above piece of diamond and gold jewelry was offered to a pretty redhead I met while visiting Las Vegas. This is the same type of story. He'd come in to visit this young woman, about 21, and developed a crush on her, which is not unusual at all. Difference is, this guy was single and so was the girl. He was actually looking for a girlfriend. After a couple of months of getting to know each other inside the club, he offered to take the redhead and her female friend to lunch. She felt pretty safe since he invited the friend. Smart move on his part, I'd say.

This lunch/shopping ritual went on several times and at one point he offered to buy her a beautiful diamond bracelet that she'd adored for some time. She tried it on, fell in love with it and he said he'd meet her the next day to purchase it. Of course, that evening he pressured her for a relationship. She wasn't interested and as you probably guessed, the bracelet is still in the store. Win some….lose some.

Six dozen roses: At a club in Colorado, a man sent an acquaintance of mine six dozen roses in all colors for no reason. Well, the reason was that he liked her and wanted to impress her. The bouquets were so large that she needed plenty of help getting them home. Imagine what the neighbors were thinking? They probably thought she robbed the florist!

While she appreciated the beautiful gesture and loved all the flowers she said it would have been better if he'd had given her a rent check, which is most likely what those roses cost him! Romantic indeed, but a little over done I think.

I'll buy You a House: Yes, a house. A man actually offered a girl a house! This in a small club in a rural area where a proposition likes this isn't all that popular. This gentleman was about fifty and had a favorite girl he'd stop in to see. Every time he'd visit he'd give her at least $200 to dance and chat with him. He would even pick her up from work along with a girl friend of hers and take them both to a casino, which was three hours away. He would pay for everything and drive them both home again, asking for nothing but the company. NOT for the house though. He wanted her to be with him, have sex with him and become his girlfriend. She politely declined the offer as she' was simply not interested in him like that. She was also quite young and wasn't about to settle down for all the wrong reasons.

Costumes: Very popular. There are people who float from club to club selling costumes and shoes. Of course they come in when the place is open and a lot of girls are working. MANY times, a customer will pay for one or more costumes for his favorite dancer, especially if she lets him help decide what she should get. I've seen girls put on a fashion show for the guy and he ends up buying everything because they "all look so great." Smart move ladies.

College Tuition: One guy paid for at least two semesters of college for a dancer. He'd also take cash advances on his credit card while at the club and give her money for books and necessities like clothes for school and gas for the car, which was brand new, by the way. He'd give her $200 or $300 each time in cash alone. Rumor had it that she was "visiting" with him once a week, but no one knows for sure. Since no names or places are mentioned, I don't think I'm gossiping, am I? I also think that might be true because it's the guy from the "I'll pay the mortgage" story.

Whatever he does....you get it free: Whatever profession the guy is in many times translates into free services and/or merchandise for the lady of his interest.

Such as:

He repairs cars: She gets her car fixed for free.

He owns an auto body shop: She gets her car painted for free.

He works at a car dealership: She gets a good deal.

He owns the car dealership: She gets a better deal.

He's a carpenter: He'll fix your house.

He's a dentist: Free bleach...no cavities.

He's a pilot: If he's got his own jet, you're all set.

He's a stockbroker: She gets great tips on the market

He's a bookie: She gets great tips on everything.

He's a doctor: No need for health insurance.

He's a massage therapist: They ALL say that.

Dream Professions:

A plastic surgeon: Boobs, lips, lipo! *I'll go with this one!*

A Jewelry store owner. Make that a chain of stores.

A wholesaler for designer shoes. Oh yeah.

A wholesaler for designer clothes. Gotta have something to go with those shoes!

THE CUSTOMERS:
Some Nice—Some, Not So Nice

Most guys frequenting clubs are just there to have a good time, look at the pretty ladies, have a drink or two, hang out with their friends and go home. Some just like the idea of being around dancers and try to get actual dates. There are no "stories" with these guys. They just come in, enjoy and leave. There are however, those who do give me stories to write about. These are the guys with different requests, fetishes and fantasies that are most definitely interesting. Unfortunately, there are also the ones that are just plain jerks. It takes all kinds. Here are some of their requests as well as some of the things they do.

Pantyhose Man: Monday night, not particularly busy and just an average night. I'd finished with a stage set when a man asked for a table dance. Before the bar was remodeled, the table dance area wasn't as private as it should have been. After all, if a gentleman pays extra for a private dance, it should be private. At this time, the private area was only secluded with scattered large plants. It was a peek-a-boo setting where others, who weren't paying the extra money, could see somewhat. There were love seats in the area as well as comfortable, easy chairs, tables and small platforms right in front of the armchairs. The platforms were for the dancer.

The gentleman hiring me for the dance appeared to be right out of an insurance office, bank or some other typical business. Neat, well groomed, probably in his late 30's or early 40's, he wore a button down shirt with a small stripe, paired with casual, cotton khaki slacks and loafer type shoes. He looked like a dressed down businessman. He had a pleasant appearance with nicely cut, light brown hair, no beard or mustache and no glasses.

He chose the love seat and invited me to sit. He sat straight ahead, while I was at the end of the love seat, at an angle, so that my knees were closer to him than my rear end. We had about two minutes of small talk, when he asked me if I'd do something for him.

He reached into a small bag and pulled out a pair of pantyhose. He requested that I put them on and dance for him. I was a bit surprised, I admit, as I don't see anything sexy in a woman dressed in nothing but a pair of pantyhose! We're not talking about thigh highs here! Looking back, it really doesn't seem that odd at all, now that I've been seasoned to all sorts of fetishes, but I wasn't quite sure how to react back then. He said he usually pays double the price for the "pantyhose dance." Money talks. He showed me where he'd cut out the crotch of the hosiery and reinforced the stitching with a sewing machine. *He did a pretty good job, I gotta say.* He assured me that this was a new pair of hose and being a woman who wears pantyhose on a regular basis I knew he was telling the truth. They come out of the package flat and if even tried on become stretched. These were definitely not worn. I agreed.

I put on the pantyhose under my little dress and stood on the platform. I stripped out of the dress and just before I actually started to dance, he pulled up his shirt a little and his pant down a little, revealing a pair of….yes…pantyhose. When he saw that the look on my face wasn't one of shock, he took off his shoes and socks and showed me his feet dressed in the pantyhose. He was so excited to be able to talk about it that his eyes lit up. He said he loved wearing them and that they made him feel comfortable. Personally, I find them binding and itchy, but then again, I don't think he shaves his legs. *Well, I don't know that for sure.*

Anyway, here I am dancing in absolutely nothing but a pair of crotchless pantyhose. Can you picture how "sexy" that is? Beige colored hose, waist to toe, with a reinforced panty that looks like a pair of shorts and a reinforced toe. No shirt, no bra, no shoes, no panties, just pantyhose.

Wouldn't be a turn on to me if I was a man, but everyone likes something different, I guess.

The funniest part of this story is this: Remember that bartender I always refer to? Well on this evening, he decided to come in as a patron, right in the middle of my pantyhose dance! Couldn't have been timed worse! Fortunately, he didn't even notice me until I came out of the private dance area fully dressed, as dressed as one gets in a strip bar that is. *He was also pretty blitzed and wouldn't remember it anyway.*

Now, every time I see a businessman, go to the bank; see a salesman, lawyer, doctor, etc. I wonder how many of them have pantyhose on. Instead of "boxers of briefs," I think, "control top or regular."

The Naked Psychologist: That would be me of course. I caught the eye of an older gentleman one evening. He was in his late fifties and went through the usual measures of stage and table dances. He looked like a typical professor from the seventies. Glasses, reddish hair, combed to the side, dress shirt completely buttoned up, dress slacks and loafers. The only thing he was missing was the sweater and bow tie. He'd pay me well and along with the dances, I would just listen to him talk about his wife and their lack of sex. He told me that he loved sex as much as the next guy but just couldn't "get it up," due to some medication he was taking for an ongoing illness.

This happened before the new medical breakthroughs for that problem. He said he'd get turned on and all, but just couldn't do anything about it. Poor guy was so depressed. I don't know why he was torturing himself in a bar with nude women!

Over the weeks, he began telling me that I was his "fantasy woman" and he needed something of mine. He bought two lace teddies and two pair of panties right off my body! He told me he'd sleep with something of mine under his pillow. How he kept this from his wife is a mystery to me. Maybe they slept in separate rooms or something.

As time went on, he did let me know that since I was his fantasy woman, maybe I could really help him with his problem and meet him somewhere for a "private show." Again, I'm no genius, but I don't think he wanted any type of a "show." After a while, he stopped coming in, then about six months later, showed up again....same story. Eventually he stopped coming in completely and one day; about two years later he popped in and announced that he'd discovered Viagra! Thank goodness for modern technology!

Tease Me Mistress, Please: This happened on a Saturday afternoon. I was on stage for the first set of the day, when a man tipped me well and asked for a private dance. No problem. He sat comfortably in the chair and the music started. He was most likely in his sixties and for the most part, the older gents like to be teased and not see it all at once. I asked him if he wanted the costume on or off. He asked me to please dance the first song with everything on.

I started the dance, teasing him all the way. He said he needed to be trained and called me "Mistress." Good thing I had the phone sex line going too or I wouldn't have known how to handle this guy's fetishes.

I told him he'd have to prove worthy. I sat in the chair opposite him and gave him my foot telling him he'd know what to do. He kissed the shoe and then the toe. Good boy. He did just what he was supposed to do. I danced the whole song with clothing on and told him what he was in store for. I ended up dancing three songs for him and never took much off. When he was a good boy, he got a flash. When he was bad, he got his hair pulled. Yeah, I know....no contact. Occasionally that rule gets forgotten...OOPS.

Socks for Sale: On a busy Friday night a rather heavyset man, I'd say in his mid to late thirties, was sitting at the stage enjoying the many girls. I was the waitress at the time. One of the girls was wearing a short, tight little dress in a shiny shade of blue, if I remember correctly. She had bare legs and wore little ruffled ankle socks with her heels. This is a good idea when wearing closed toe shoes as it prevents feet from sweating and looks cute. Guys seem to like it, especially this one. He asked for a private dance and told her he liked her best because she was the only one wearing closed shoes. She did one dance for him and sat for a minute to put the dress back on and chat. He paid her for another dance, but didn't want her to dance. He just wanted to rub her feet.

She stayed dressed and seated for the next song while he caressed her tootsies. He did try to put her feet on his lap but she didn't allow it. After two private dances, he offered her twenty dollars for her three-dollar ankle socks. She said yes and he tipped her an extra ten. At the time, table dances were only ten dollars each, so she made a quick fifty. Not bad, and she got a foot massage to top it off!

Just Let Me Look At Your Feet: This guy was young, probably late twenties, chocolate skinned and dressed like a rapper on TV. Nice appearance and he had on some great cologne. Now I'm not stereotyping, but many men who are African American or Hispanic appreciate a nice tush and great curves. This guy was complimentary about everything, but focused on wanting to look at my feet. He kept asking for a closer view. I sat on the bar and showed him my feet! He loved looking at the red toe polish through the fishnet black stockings. He asked me to take off a shoe. Okay. *My feet were hurting anyway.* He was thrilled with the feet and had fun simply touching them. I'd have to say he was actually admiring them. I let him touch my toes and left him smiling.

Drinks For Everyone!: This guy, mid forties, gray hair and mustache was just as friendly as could be. His thing was to come in and sit at the bar, talk to all the ladies and buy drinks for them. No tips for dancing, didn't go to the stage, no table dances. He'd just buy all the dancers lots of drinks and some they didn't really want.

He said his intentions were simple, to get everyone drunk! He did a good job and many of the ladies just let him go ahead with it! That's all he wanted to do. He didn't try to take anyone home or take advantage of anyone. Just wanted everyone to have a good time. His bar tab was unbelievable! Sometimes the owner would get irritated with him cause he got all the dancers smashed! I can understand that. After all, here are a bunch of giddy ladies, stumbling around when they're supposed to be graceful! Neat guy though.

Pantyholic: At a club I was working in, all the girls in the back room were talking about a man who bought everyone's panties. I didn't get into the conversation, but listened to them say they each told him twenty dollars per pair. He'd generally offer thirty for the panties and a private dance. One girl was curious about who he was and asked his description. My cell phone rang so I didn't hear the rest.

Went back to work, went on stage, did my set and came down. I had just stepped down when a younger man in his early thirties came over and said hello. *Early thirties IS younger to me, you know.* He asked what was written on my panties. I told him it was the name of a club in another state, a souvenir. He asked to buy them. It was Pantyman! I told him no, but that I had another pair of white ones in the dressing room he might like. He asked how much, I told him twenty, he offered thirty with a private dance just like the girls said he would, and that was that.

The underwear went on, the dance went well, he got his panties and I got my thirty dollars. Later in the evening I saw him in the private dance area with the other girl who had been asking about him. Seems he had to have a pair of everyone's panties. He'd come into the club every two or three weeks to see if there are any new girls and buy their underwear. Must have quite a collection. I'd like to know if he labels them or just puts them in a drawer. If I ever see him again, I'm gonna ask.

Ladies Welcome

Many people ask if women come into strip bars and why. First of all, yes they do, and it's becoming more popular than ever now. They come for many reasons. Among them:

Some are simply gay or bisexual. I see many couples come in hand in hand and go right to the stage. Many times they will put money up in the middle of them both. For some reason, the couples are often more generous than the singles. The money in the middle means that the dance is for both of them. I have personally danced for couples as well as women alone and they have always been courteous, kind and polite. Guys: You might think this is the perfect situation, the dream that every man wants. You know, his girl to enjoy another woman, perhaps even bringing one home. Sounds good in theory, but in reality the same problems apply as in any other situation. At times, three can be a crowd.

Girls go to nice strip bars to meet single men. There's a local bar near where I live that's one big party on the weekends. There are guys at the stage, girls at the stage, couples at the stage and guys and girls just hanging out having drinks. One night I ran into some young ladies I knew, early twenties and asked them what they were doing there. They said they heard it was a fun bar and tried it. They liked it and found that there were all kinds of eligible men, many with good professions. It takes some money to have a good time in these places. Cover charges, highly priced drinks, money for the dancers and the gentlemen always buy the ladies their drinks. It adds up fast. For the more open-minded women who aren't the jealous type, this situation is great.

It's safe. A girl in a strip bar is guaranteed to be safe. The guys don't often get out of hand because they can't. They'll get thrown out. There are always bouncers as in any other bar, but if a lady needs an escort to her car, the bouncer will usually oblige.

No one gives the girls a hard time. Ladies, we've all experienced this one. You're at a dance club having a good time and some guy gives you the eye or makes a comment. His half or totally drunk girlfriend sees it and gets mad…AT YOU! *Like it's your fault?* I say yell at him. Anyway, that's not the usual case. I've had young girls try to start arguments or make rude comments. Once a girl accidentally "brushed" by me and when she caught her guy looking, got mad and tried to pick a fight. She was thrown out…he he. The above situation seldom happens in a strip bar. The guys are in there specifically TO look at women, and any female in there knows it so there's no problems. Whether they're looking at a girl on stage, a pretty waitress or you, it's all okay.

One more reason….terribly selfish, but true. The guys always buy the drinks! Women rarely pay for anything. *Hey, I'm just being truthful.* For you guys….try a ladies night when the entertainment consists of male dancers. Dress nice and float around the perimeter. No one will know if you're with the production, waiting for your lady, or just visiting. Either way, the women will be buying you the drinks.

Out Of Hand Customers:

Do the customers ever get out of hand? In two words….oh yeah, although not very often. I've seen less trouble in strip bars than in regular bars, far less. When they do get out of control, it's most likely because they do something they're not supposed to do with respect to the dancers. Fighting with other guys due to over drinking isn't generally the case as is in the local pool table bar.

There are many ways to handle situations. Call a bouncer or manager and have the guy thrown out, or deal with him. It really depends on the client, the club, the girl and the attitudes and moods of those involved.

Following are some personal accounts and others are from girls I know and/or have asked.

Show Me More: This is an example of what a guy should not do in a strip bar and what can happen if he does. For as long as I can remember, it's always been a one-dollar bill that's put up at most stages in most average clubs for a dance. No one seems to take into consideration that a dollar certainly isn't worth what it was ten years ago, never mind thirty, yet it's still only a dollar that's put up. Now what do you guys expect for that dollar? A little show. Some men apparently think that they deserve a full five minutes of exactly what they want.

A friend of mine was on stage, went over to a customer and started a little show for that dollar bill he was waving. She did her little dance but he wanted more, and he wasn't nice about it. "Bend over, I want to see your ass." She was nice and bent over a little. "Bend over more." was his request, or rather, demand. She bent over a little more, beginning to get aggravated with the guy. "Bring your tits closer." This requires getting on ones knees to bring ones breasts to eye level of the customer. Apparently, she had a plan.

She got face to face with him and he said: "After that, bring your pussy closer." She'd had it with him now. She smiled and said "For a dollar?" Now if he had any sense at all, with his demanding attitude, he would have put up a ten or a twenty. Instead he put up another dollar and said "There!" She got up, sat on the little ledge and started to raise her leg as if she was going to show him everything, very close up. As he moved his face closer, she "accidentally biffed him in the head with her heel" as she put it. "Oh sir, I'm so sorry! Are you okay?" she said with a smirk. She picked up the dollar and walked away.

The guy sat quietly the rest of the time and I'm sure didn't try that on another girl.

A Nasty Boy: A girl I worked with in her mid twenties had been dancing for only two months, when a client who'd been seen before came in. I was the waitress on that night and recognized him right away. Tall, very tall, dark hair, well-groomed and about thirty to thirty-five years old. He tipped me pretty well as well as the fairly new girl on stage. He asked her for a table dance. No problem. The five foot three brunette stood five foot eight with her heels yet was still considerably shorter than he was. They moved to the back table near the second stage, which was not in use that evening.

The pretty brunette began dancing for him and turned around to give him a nice "rear" view of the dance. She was in a little short dress with nothing else on except high heels. When she turned around to face him, she was greeted with his hand on his penis! The dancer, still new at this wasn't quite sure what to do, but had to think fast. Was he trying to initiate her with a shock? Did he really think she'd be impressed by his very rude behavior? Or was he just a jerk. He kept telling her to "touch it….look at it." Now if the bouncer saw this before the dancer decided to handle it herself, the customer would have been thrown out with his pants down around his knees. The bouncer took crap like that from no one.

She simply turned to him and smiled so that to everyone else, including myself, everything appeared to be fine. She told him to "put that damn thing away, NOW!" No arguments. He did as she said and left the club abruptly, probably to avoid the possibility of a face off with the bouncer. I'm not sure how often I saw him in there again. Maybe once or twice and that's it. I wonder if he found someone who actually wanted to look at it and touch it, but somehow I don't think so. What a jerk.

Seventy-Five and HORNY: This was a weekday night at 7:00 PM. The shifts were changing and the night girls were arriving as the day girls left. At this time of evening in this little pleasant club, there are more girls than there were guys in the place. I was one of the night girls. Noticing an older man sitting by a table, alone, I smiled and said hello. He motioned for me to come over and sit with him. He ordered me a drink immediately and began chatting. I found out he was seventy-five but looked good for his age. He also happened to mention that he's impotent and just enjoying the beautiful women to try and get things going again. *Haven't we heard this before?*

He asked me if I'd do a private dance for him even before my first stage set. No problem. All went well, except that he was a little "handsy," however quite controllable. He seemed pleased and soon after asked me if we could make an "arrangement" to meet somewhere so I could "help" him with his problem. I smiled, mumbled something to avoid an answer and walked him to the front of the bar again. These situations get a little touchy (pardon the pun) because if you just plain tell the guy off you could be losing future money, so you play it for a while and see what happens.

He'd come back often and purchase private dances with most of the other girls as well. He'd keep coming back to me, which is why I'm glad I didn't tell him off. On another occasion, he announced that he really was horny. The guy was SO grabby this time! He tried putting his hands everywhere. What to do? Well, I could have easily called someone who would have scolded him, and/or thrown him out. I chose to turn around, hold his hands up while I danced for him an told him to be a "good boy." It was a milder way to control this over zealous older man, and still keep the cash flowing. Hope he found what he was looking for!

Watch That Finger!: A male friend who was at a strip bar with one of his buddies related this story to me. They were at the stage, tipping girls and drinking a beer, which was nothing out of the ordinary. My friend's buddy, who we'll call "Buddy," asked for a table dance in the VIP room. He went into the room and within two minutes was out again. He sat down and my friend commented on how that must have been the shortest private dance in history. He asked "Buddy" why it was so short. Buddy just said he didn't know and went back to looking at girls on stage again.

Not a minute later, a very large bouncer came over to the two guys and asked, "Which one of you is Buddy?" Looking straight at my friend. He shook his head, pointed his finger and said, "Uh…he is." The big bouncer firmly put his hand on Buddy's shoulder and said, "I'm afraid you'll have to leave now." My friend gave him a smirk and asked, "Now what did we do in there?" My friend was nice enough to leave with his "buddy" and as they walked out he confessed, "Well, she was dancing and she turned around and bent over. I figured she wanted me to do something so I stuck my finger in her butt."

My friend didn't know whether to laugh or smack the guy for being so dumb. Needless to say, "Buddy" wasn't welcome in that bar anymore.

Dangerous Customers

Unfortunately, this does happen from time to time. Customers can become bothersome, obsessed and even dangerous. In reality, obsessions can and do happen to anyone, and certainly isn't limited to the adult industry, but these stories are from and about dancers.

I'll pinch you: This happened to a friend of mine. She finished her shift, had an average night and left to go home. Nothing unusual had happened that particular evening. No one made any advances towards her, given her a large amount of money or any exceptional attention. She left the bar and went home. Fortunately for her, she went to her boyfriend's house that night. As she pulled up, she heard a tap on her window. Startled, she looked up and saw a client from the club glaring into her partially opened window.

She asked him what he wanted and he said, "You!" Not the right answer. He said he followed her from the club and wanted to know if she lived there. She said that she didn't but that her boyfriend was inside waiting for her. She was smart enough to say she was already running fifteen minutes late and that he'd be looking for her. While she was talking to him, she glanced at her passenger door to see if she'd locked it. She had. She was also smart enough to had already locked her door, but the window was opened enough for him to get his hand in if he wanted to. She was feeling a little panicky but didn't want him to know it so she tried to talk him away.

After a couple of minutes of conversation he offered her money for sex. Right there in the car. Now she had to think fast. Should she start the car and go? He might follow. Scream? Hit him? She opted to hit the horn and yell for her boyfriend. This freaked the guy out. Before he ran away, he pinched her. Yeah, that's right. He pinched her hard on the arm. That'll show ya lady!!! He was never heard from or seen again.

In case you're wondering why she didn't just call her boyfriend on her cell phone, this happened way back in the seventies. Some of us were already adults back then when there were no cell phones.

Maybe I Have a Cock: This is really funny. A girl, working at a topless only bar had an encounter with an over zealous client. She was a tall, natural blond with the biggest blue eyes on earth. Nice round behind and thick long hair that fell over some very nice breasts. No mistaking that she was a girl.

One early evening, after a day shift, she brought a few things out to her car and was planning to come back inside when a client who'd been in the club approached her. He'd actually left about twenty minutes before, saying goodbye to this pretty blond whom he'd been quite generous with. She'd been tipped well on stage and he took three table dances. Not that unusual. He said goodbye at the club and that he'd be back the next time she worked. Obviously he waited for her in the parking lot, knowing that her shift was about to end.

She closed her car door and turned to go back into the club when he came up to ask her to dinner. She politely declined, saying that she was going to meet her boyfriend right away. He pleaded, almost sounding pathetic, now adding some sexual comments. She got nervous. The bouncer was inside and this bar was in a remote area, not in the city where there are lots of people around. What to do?

This girl thought faster than I could ever dream of. She's got a great sense of humor and used it to her advantage. In a sweet voice she said to him, "So, you want to take me out to dinner and then go back to a hotel for some fun, right?" "Oh yeah baby!" was his comment. All of a sudden her voice changed to a very deep baritone. "But how do you know that I wasn't born a boy? Maybe I have a cock!" The guy's face faded to white, he turned and literally ran to his car. I don't know about you, but I laughed for ten minutes straight when I heard this one!

I'll Huff & I'll Puff & I'll Burn the Place Down: A girl who'd been dancing a few years had a boyfriend who suddenly decided he didn't want her dancing anymore. He told her to stop but she didn't feel she needed to be told what to do and kept her job.

The boyfriend said that if she didn't stop working there, he'd burn the place to the ground. Okay, whatever. Well, this guy wasn't kidding. He apparently lit the place and it certainly did burn, but not to the ground. All that ended up happening was that the insurance covered the damages to the club and now it looks much better and newer!

Unfortunately, he was only questioned and never charged because they didn't have enough evidence. Where are those forensic guys when you need em?

I'll Follow You Home: Yes, this does happen, sad to say, but as I've mentioned before, it can happen to anyone at any job.

A girl left the bar when a guy pulled out very shortly after she did and appeared to be going in her direction. He was close behind her on the highway and the reason she even noticed anything was that there's little traffic in the area, especially late at night. She changed lanes, so did he. She slowed down, so did he. She sped up, so did he. Now she knew he was following her. Not a very good stalker, I must say. He'd make a terrible detective!

Although nervous, panic had not set in. She slowed down a little and pressed the "9" and the "1" button on her cell phone and proceeded to get off at a different exit rather than her usual one. She drove on some side streets just to make sure he was really following her. Personally I wouldn't have done that. It was too dark and too risky. He was following. Entering at all night gas station she pressed the other "1" on her phone, calling the local police. Unfortunately, the guy must have caught on because he bolted. At least a description of the man and the car was obtained. In such a small town, he'd be pretty stupid to come back. Then again, we're not talking about the sharpest knife in the drawer anyway.

Long story short, he never came into the bar again, she got a FID card and carried mace from then on.

THE GIRLS:

Want to know more about the girls who work at these places? They do vary, believe me. From the young age of 18 and on up, tall, short, thin, chubby and in between. Plain to glamorous. Small "A" cup breasts to triple "Z." Nice to bitchy.

Myths and Truths

Following are some commonly asked questions by men and women concerning the girls who work as dancers. I will answer based on first hand knowledge of what I've seen.

Are all strippers also escorts? *Nice way of saying "prostitutes."* I hate to put it out there like this, but many people do have that opinion. I ought to know. I've been asked many times by all types of men, "how much" it would cost to "take this elsewhere," or "get a massage." Is this an insult? Yes and No. After all, it IS the sex industry but that shouldn't give everyone out there the idea that anyone who takes their clothes off for a living will also sell their bodies. Some do, some don't, but you don't have to be a stripper to sell sex for money.

There are strippers who will take it elsewhere for a price. What I've seen most is a customer who pursues a particular girl with gifts and/or money at the club. She might agree to spend some time with him and end up with nice new clothes, a vacation, cash, etc. Is this prostituting? Draw your own conclusion. How does anyone know that in these situations, the lady involved might not really enjoy spending time with the gentleman? There are also times when guy just wants a "trophy date," where there's simply a pretty girl on his arm. Also, if we're not there with them, how can anyone know if there's even sex involved?

Personally, I don't think it's for anybody to judge. After all, how many women out there have a different "boyfriend" every couple of months and end up with the same material benefits? Think about it.

$20 Hookers? There are strippers who will go out to a parking lot and trade some instant satisfaction for $20. Is this prostituting? I guess so, but there is another reason why they do this. There are always and I mean always, serious drugs involved in these cases. The issue isn't that of a "stripper turned hooker," it's one of drug abuse. How many drug addicts out there do the same thing and never walk into a strip bar? Plenty.

Most strippers are NOT escorts and know their trade well enough to make the money they need in the club doing what they're paid to do. Dance and entertain. It's a job and just a job. Acting like a sex toy on stage to entertain is the image that is being portrayed inside the club, not outside. Just think of it this way. If every actor we've seen in a movie who plays a killer really were, we'd have a lot more nuts than we already have roaming the streets! It's just a job.

*Note: I'm in no way putting down professional escorts. That's also a job, but we're concentrating on dancers.

All strippers must be sluts: Another good one. To be honest, I must say that this is the opinion of mainly women. Women who don't know strippers and who have more than likely have never entered a strip bar. I know, I used to be one of them. My reason? Jealousy due to low self-confidence. I admit it. I always wondered what it would be like to be a dancer but didn't have the body at the time for the job. I weighed less than 85 pounds in my twenties, and obviously didn't have the confidence either. So I tried to find something "wrong" with dancers without ever giving them a chance. Here's how it really is. Some strippers are the biggest sluts there are and some are the girls next door. Just like in any other profession.

First hand, I've seen more ladies in a rock and roll bar, who have very nice office jobs or professions, get totally drunk and end up behind the clubs with one of the band members they just met. They weren't just talking or smoking a cigarette believe me. These girls would be considered the "nice girls" because of their professions being approved by society. Boy they sure let their hair down on weekends! Also, some of the office girls were just as calm as their jobs. It's the same with dancers. Some work all day and go home to their husbands, kids or textbooks, making a stop at the grocery store on the way home and some party all night. Some are just single and enjoying life while others get completely crazy.

I once encountered a very young stripper, 19, who blatantly came up to me and said she was flirting with the guy I liked and was going to try to take him home with her. She would have acted like that whether she was a stripper or an accountant. That's just how she was. Point is: Strippers are people. People come from all different backgrounds, ethics and morals regardless of what they do for a living. Just watch any talk show. By the way, do you think I let that young girl get away with talking like that to me? Not in this lifetime. She made sure she mentioned that this guy had a thing for blondes and I was a brunette at the time. I told her that although true, I also knew that he only dated older women and that she was twenty years too young for him. If she didn't believe me…just ask him. That shut her up quickly.

Do all strippers take drugs? The bar scene is party central, whether it's a strip bar or a country western bar. Drugs are always available. That's a fact. I must admit, I've seen much more drug use among dancers than in a lot of other professions. It's not always to the extreme though and not everyone does it. Because of the party like atmosphere, it's acceptable to be a little tipsy on the job. Drinks flow freely and sometimes drugs follow. Can you imagine going to your local bank and having all the tellers acting silly as they sipped their vodka and oj? This behavior is certainly not suitable for that type of work. It may very well be going on, but isn't out in the open as in the adult entertainment industry where there's just no need to hide it. Also, how do we know how many people in what society accepts as "respectable" professions, over drink and use drugs outside of work?

The problem is this: Some people have a tough time remembering that they are at a job and that day after day of drinking and drugging will mess with their health, mind and age them rapidly. Many others however, have the good sense to keep the partying to a minimum and stay away from the drugs. It's just not worth it. Unfortunately, that lifestyle will catch up with you, no matter what.

Don't you need to be drunk or high to get on stage and strip? Good question. It's sad that there are some that need to drink to get the courage to dance. In my opinion, *(I know, I'm full of opinions, aren't I?),* if you have to get drunk to get on stage, don't get on stage! Waitress, bartend, whatever, but don't dance if you can't handle it. It's not for everyone.

I personally know a young woman who is just gorgeous. Beautiful face, hair, killer body and perfectly toned. I asked her one day why she busted her rear end bartending when she could double her money easily by dancing. Said it just wasn't for her and she'd have to get drunk to do it. I give her credit. Although bartenders, especially ones that look like her, make good money, she'd make better money stripping, but she knows her own limits. She'd rather work extra days bartending than drink just to get a job done. She's one smart young lady.

Is it always just for the money? Aren't all jobs? It's a job where an attractive woman can make the same amount of money in one night as she can in one week working at a different profession. Some girls are able to pay their way through college and still have time to study by working two nights at a bar rather than forty hours somewhere else. Some are supporting their kids; others are just getting by and some just blow their money. In all cases, money is the key here. Is it always for the money? Just ask any stripper if she'd do it for free? You already know the answer.

Do all strippers have, or need huge breasts? Definitely not. I've seem girls with an A cup make plenty of money. However, remember that this is a very superficial business and as much as some would not like to believe it, breasts DO sell. Those same slender young ladies with A cups who make good money, definitely make more money when they enhance the breasts to a C cup. Doesn't matter if they're "fake" or not. The guys don't usually care. I must say that most guys I've asked say they like average sized breasts. This maybe true, but when a dancer gets on stage with gigantic breasts, the money comes up. The really huge, watermelon breasts attract more attention than admiration although, believe me, they DO have their place in the industry, a very good one at that.

Girl Stories:
Some Funny—Some Sad

I'd like to let you in on some of the interesting stories that happen with the girls. From the funny things that go on between the ladies to some of the scary incidents that they have had to encounter.

Phone Fun At The Club: I was working a night shift and it was relatively early. It was that time of night where there weren't too many customers. A phone call came in to my sex line while I was in the dressing room and I figured I'd have time to take it. He'd called before, but I didn't have notes so I wasn't sure exactly what he was into. There were two other girls in the dressing room at the time and I told them I was about to take a sex call. I offered to go into the ladies room, but they wanted to listen. Okay with me.

When I called the client back and told him he'd have to refresh my memory, he said he wanted to be humiliated and dildo trained. No problem. The two girls listened while I told him he was bad for not wearing red lipstick and he'd have to do that next time. Imagine how funny it was when the door opened and two more girls came in, with the two already in there giggling and "shhhhising." Now picture a petite, 100 pound blonde on the phone telling this guy he's "nothing but a slutty whore, a little sissy and a bitch." I told him there was a room full of girls and I was going to tell them all what a little nasty bitch he was. I made him moan loud while shoving a dildo in his butt. I held the phone away from my ear so that everyone could hear, including myself there were six now. They were cracking up and we really all had a good time.

Now, I don't think anyone was actually laughing at him, just at the situation in general. They were amazed at how I simply ended the call, told him to have a nice evening, hung up, and went back to refreshing my makeup.

From "A" to "DD": This is about a girl I met when I started to waitress at a strip bar. I would never have the "b's" to do what she did and I give her a lot of credit for going after what she wanted.

This was a "table dance" club in the mid 90's, with $10 dances right at your table. The girls had to wear evening gowns or cocktail dresses only and there was no "floor work." They didn't touch the floor with their knees or rear end. All dancing was done standing up. The atmosphere in this place was definitely on the classy side with uniformed waitresses, bartenders and no plastic cups anywhere. The girls who worked as dancers were all very good looking.

One slender brunette would walk around to customers and ask for a table dance, just like everyone else. She made a nice appearance, on the natural side and wore gowns that were flattering to her figure. Now keep in mind, that's fine to do, but it all comes off, so what's underneath has to look good too.

When they gave her the money and she stripped for them, her size "A" breasts literally fell out of her dress. Nothing wrong with an "A" cup, even for a stripper, but they were just plain flabby. One would guess she'd had children, gained and lost a lot of weight in her breasts, or had a weight problem at one time. Being the waitress, I heard the comments and I'm sure she did also. She wasn't stupid, far from it. Most times, the comments weren't very nice.

She worked at the bar for maybe six months and said she was going to travel, stripping at different clubs in different states. No one heard from her for a while, until a couple of years later.

Same club, two years later, Friday night. In comes a summer bleached blonde with long extensions to her butt and at least double D sized breasts, maybe even triple D's. Guess who? She'd gained about 20 pounds and wasn't so thin, dyed her hair and obviously did something with her breasts. She changed her stage name to something like "Lollie Pop" and was touring! It was the same friendly girl, just in a totally different package. I give her so much credit for going out there and getting what she set out to do. I hope she's doing well and set for life!

In The Locker: A twenty-one year old girl I worked with one night told this story to me. We'll call her Sally. She'd come from another club that was temporarily closed down for renovations. I've been there so I know some of the things that go on. This was most definitely true.

Sally was working one evening and went into the dressing room. The lockers were a good size and she saw a girl actually sitting in one of them. Sally looked closer to see what the girl was doing and saw that she was smoking crack/cocaine inside the locker. Sally thought fast, picked up her lock, slammed the door to the locker shut and padlocked it, with the girl inside! Then she went over to the owner, handed him the key to her locker and told him to go into the dressing room and open the door. He'd find a dancer sitting inside, smoking crack.

The owner did check and the girl inside the locker was immediately thrown out and told never to come back. No, they don't call the police for stuff like that. Just get rid of the bad apple.

*Note: Like I said, crazy things went on in that place and the girl telling the story was no exception. She proudly announced being an ex cocaine dealer who sold her drugs in that club.

A Powder Story (funny): This is one of the dumbest of my moments. Well, I think "naive" would be a better word. Judge for yourself.

I was visiting a local strip bar, the same one as the girl in the locker story, with a guy who I was friends with. I knew some of the dancers on a very casual basis only. One came up to me and said hello. Hello back. Then she leaned over to my ear and asked me, "Do you have any powder?" I looked down and saw that she was wearing sandals and no stockings. I said, "Gee, no, I'm sorry, I don't have any with me." She responded, "It's not for me." Now I'm confused. Why would she ask for powder if she wasn't going to use it? (*I thought she was referring to baby powder*) I ignored the comment. She then asked me to ask my friend if he had any. Really confused now, I told her I didn't think he had any either. She was persistent and kept telling me to just go over and ask him. OK, why not.

I walked over to my friend, who I'll call Peter. He was talking to another guy in the bar. I called his name, but he didn't answer. Engrossed in his conversation, I called him again but still no response. I could see the girl impatiently waiting for me to ask him about the powder. *Boy, her feet must really have been sweaty!* Finally, I pulled on his shirt and yelled, "Peter! That girl over there wants to know if you have any powder!" I've never seen a hand go over a mouth faster. "What?" I thought, I just asked a simple question.

He took me over to a private area and said he needed to give me a lesson. It went something like this, "In here, when people talk about rails, they're not talking about cho-cho trains. And when they're talking about white lines, they don't mean the lines in the road. And when they're talking about powder, it's NOT baby powder. And one more thing…..When people say it's snowing, don't go outside and look!" Good thing I never told him that once someone did say it was snowing in July and I really

DID go outside and look! Turned out that the impatient girl was a total cocaine/crack addict.

Another Play On Words: Yeah, I did it again. This actually happened before the powder thing. I was a waitress this time at a different bar. I went to a table with two guys, I'd say in their mid twenties to take their order. They ordered two beers and asked me for "blow." Well, I hadn't been a waitress long but had just heard of a shot called a "blow job," which is what I assumed they wanted. I asked if they wanted whipped cream on the top of the shot. They looked confused and said, "No, we want some blow." I told them politely that I'd heard of the "blow job" shot, but that was it and that I'd ask the bartender if he had any. One guy practically took my arm off and snapped, "No, don't ask the bartender!"

Now I was a little annoyed. How could I get them what they wanted if they wouldn't tell me what it was? That's exactly what I said to them. I asked if it was whiskey, scotch, or what? I told them I couldn't help them if they wouldn't cooperate. I walked away to get their beers and mentioned it to the bartender. He walked over to the guys himself, with me standing there, gave them their drinks and told them never to ask a waitress for cocaine again. Oh….that's what they meant? Well, at least I knew now.

Note: Before this job, I was a homemaker and only worked outside the home for once a week cleaning jobs. This might explain why I had no clue about the real world. Now maybe if they were using the drug terminology of the sixties, when I was a teenager, I might have caught on. I also found out that there was plenty of "blow" inside that bar and everyone knew it. Everyone but me, I guess.

Just One More Time: I have two reasons for telling this one. First, because I think my initiation into the drug lingo is nothing short of hilarious and second, because it shows the effects that the drugs have on some of these ladies.

Still the same bar as the powder story. You're probably wondering why I kept going there? My friend who did my body guarding for bachelor parties liked one of the dancers so we'd frequent the place often. I went to the dressing room to talk to the girl that my friend liked. A different girl had a cigarette lighter and was "fiddling" with it. I thought she was trying to fix it. She put something into a part of the lighter, took another lighter and lit it. Then she started smoking it. I looked at her completely confused and she said, "You don't see this, OK?" My brilliant comment was, "I don't even know what that is." She could tell by my facial expression that I was being truthful. I'd never seen anyone "smoke" a lighter before but the genius in me figured out that it must be some kind of drug. See we didn't have "crack" in the sixties so I didn't know much about it. Then I added, "I can't get high or anything from that, can I?" She said no.

After leaving the bar and sitting in the car with my friend, waiting for the heat to come on, I casually mentioned the lighter incident. I told him that when she smoked it made a "crackle, crackle" sound. He just looked at me like I had three eyes and said, "That's crack, dummy." Bright comment number two, "Oh, so that's why they call it crack!"

The girl smoking it was in her late twenties and had four kids, none of which lived with her. If I'm not mistaken, they were all if not most, separated from each other, living in different places. How sad to have four of your own creations and live a life for crack instead of for them. She was funny, witty, and bright. Too bad that the drugs ruled her life. The girl in the "powder" story also chose drugs over her kids.

Note: Reading this, you may conclude that I'm not as sympathetic with these women as some might think I should be, but that's because I am a mother and nothing, I mean NOTHING comes before my children. It is my opinion that since we brought them into the world, it's our responsibility to take care of them. Fathers are no exception. Go to counseling, a rehab, call a friend or family member, whoever and whatever it takes to be okay and take care of your kids. I do however have empathy for addicted people, just not sympathy. I'm fortunate enough not to know what it's like.

Completely Opposite: This is the complete opposite of the above story and is to emphasize that not everyone uses drugs and has no purpose to their life.

While working one night, in came two very young girls, not even twenty-one yet. Both had black hair, one long, one short and chocolate skin. They got dressed and made up like any other dancer, but before they went on stage, they took out their lap top computers and got them ready. After their set, they didn't socialize and drink with the customers, or ask for private dances. Instead, they rushed back into the dressing room and started typing.

Turns out, they were both college students and both had papers due the next day. They were busy working all night in between stage sets to get their projects finished. Smart, goal oriented ladies who just wanted to make some money to get through college. Good for them. I hope they make plenty of money and get honors at the same time!

A funny note: They were in the room during the phone sex call. One of them accidentally typed "pussy" in her report. It's a good thing she caught it or her professor might have fainted!

A Thief In The Dressing Room: I told you the stories aren't all nice. Not only have I heard plenty of stories about things being stolen, but also I've experienced it myself. On my list are: Makeup, expensive perfume, costumes, one that was custom made and expensive, another that wasn't expensive. The less expensive one I made myself and put a lot of work into it. I've had countless CD's stolen from a club in which we brought our own music in and of course, money. You don't leave your money unattended for a minute. There was one place where the barmaid was kind enough to tell me she'd hold my money for me. I told her I'd just put it in the locker and she said it wasn't a good idea. Why not? I had a lock. She brought me into the dressing room and pointed out that if someone had the locker above me, they could easily open it and get into the locker underneath. The lockers were actually more like large drawers. Guess I don't have the mind of a thief so I never thought of it. I willingly gave her my money to hold. Can't remember her name, but I'm ever grateful.

Another Thief: This was a young girl I worked with one night and even though the things stolen weren't worth thousands of dollars, they were worth something to me. Also, it was the WAY she took them that really pissed me off.

This was someone who was very friendly and said she enjoyed working with me. We actually went on stage together the entire night. She complemented my costume, the one that I made myself and even commented on my perfume. When I got home that night, they were both gone. The perfume was expensive, but more than that, my son had given it to me for a present so it meant a lot and she knew it. Should have figured out not to trust her when she mentioned that she used to "sell cocaine" at a strip bar that we both knew. "Used to" is the past, right? Well, this anorexic, worn out looking girl was only twenty-one. Come to find out she even had kids, who didn't live with her. Go figure…. In Jan. of 2002 she was still in my area. I Hope I never see her with my outfit on…Sparks will fly.

Sad, But So True: I met and worked with a most exquisite looking young girl. Blonde, average height, slender, gorgeous face, legs, body, etc. Her breasts had been "done," but they looked so natural it was amazing. Just beautiful and only twenty-one. She made plenty of money on stage and had guys lined up for private dances. Wouldn't you think she'd be a happy young woman, saving her money for the future and enjoying life? Wrong. She was a young mother of a five-year-old…. Yeah, that's right, a five year old and just miserable. Not because of her child, but because of her self esteem. This girl would constantly talk about how "fat" she was and how she "jiggled." She saw many of the other girls as "beautiful," but not herself. I felt for her and the "mom" in me kicked in.

She admitted to having an eating disorder and would throw up if she "ate too much." Said that it was the only way to stay thin. She told me that all the girls in her family were fat by her age and she didn't want to be that way. I can understand her feelings but it was her self-esteem that kept her this way, not her fear of fat.

One day, she came in and was really tired from being up and out all night. I replied that I understood how you could lose track of time when you're having fun. She said it wasn't because of a loss of time, but rather the use of cocaine all night as well as other drugs. The first thing that crossed my mind was "Where was the five year old and who was caring for this little kid?" I decided then and there to put "mom" away. She was too messed up for me to handle and wasn't looking for help anyway. If she keeps up this lifestyle she really will get old and worn before her time and look it, which is what she fears most.

"I'll Shoot You In The Knee:" This was the comment of a really bitchy dancer who should receive the "attitude of the year" award. This small club was one of two and she much preferred to work at the larger one. Everyone was required to put time into the smaller place and she was not happy about it. Come to think of it, she wasn't happy about anything. Tall, sophisticated brunette with a great body, pretty face and a good dancer but oh so nasty!

She had a lot of expensive costumes, and being new to the business and trying to be friendly, I politely suggested that she lock it because there was a lot of theft. With a rude look she commented that she had a gun and that if anyone took anything, she'd shoot them in the knee. She commented that the knee would be the worst place to shoot a dancer. That way, the girl could never work again. She said it with such anger too! What a head case! I never spoke to her again, not out of fear, but for the fact that

I feel she wasn't worth speaking to. I wonder if she had a license for this alleged gun?

She also crossed the line when she gave a death look to a sweet, beautiful eighteen-year-old girl. It was my daughter, who was picking me up at the time. "What's the matter honey? Feel you're getting old and can't handle a young, fresh girl around you? Afraid of some competition?" I only thought this and wasn't about to start anything. Unfortunately, that's most likely how she viewed things. Too bad. How sad. Maybe if she had cut down on her drinking and use of cocaine, she'd look fresh and young even at forty? No, I'm not gossiping, I saw it.

From Mommie To Dancer: (A nice, short story) this girl impressed me because of her good attitude. A rather wholesome, healthy looking brunette with good looks and a very welcome smile. She'd put her makeup and costumes on like everyone else, but her conversations revolved mostly around her three beautiful children. All close in age, all the same sex and all young. She was working as a dancer to put money away to buy a house for herself and children. Separated from her significant other, the father of the kids, she was making it on her own, and doing a good job.

This is a woman who deserves credit. The parties and drugs are out there, but her main concern was for her kids, as it should be. However, I've personally seen so many stories go the other way, where the kids live with someone else and mom and/or dad are just partying all the time. I hope she gets a big, beautiful home someday with someone nice to share it with.

A Psyche Major: One younger girl, about 21, was a college student majoring in Psychology. Being twenty-one and a stripper is enough for people not to take you seriously. She made every effort to "show off" her brains with impressive words and making sure everyone knew she was a serious person. It really was cute, I thought. Best part it, she used the guys as her study material.

She'd work a private dance for someone and then psychoanalyze him! It was great. I'm sure she got plenty of material in the bar to get her degree!

In disguise: Just a little story that I thought was interesting. While I was a waitress, one of the dancers did this total transformation that was just amazing. She'd walk into the bar in jeans or a jogging suit with sneakers and a tee or sweatshirt. Her hair was chin length and a dirty blond and she stood about five foot four inches. When she'd come up from the dressing room, she was totally different. She wore a long red wig that was a mass of cascading curls with bangs, and her very high heels added six inches to her height. Wearing a lot of makeup and green contact lenses to change her naturally blue eyes this girl looked like a different person altogether. The first time I saw her walk in and out, I didn't even know who she was.

I don't know her reason for doing that but it's not a bad idea. No customer would ever follow her 'cause they'd be watching the dressing room door looking for the redhead to come up. She'd be long gone! Think I'll try that sometime, somewhere, just for ha ha's.

Teacher By Day—Dancer by night. This tall, pretty lady in her early thirties with very long silky, straight, reddish brown hair was a fourth grade teacher by day. She traveled an hour and a half each way on the weekends to dance. She said she did it because she wanted to earn extra money. Goes to show you that the people responsible for the education of our children certainly do not get paid enough! She was very nice.

OOPS! It's a Wig! Ooooh…this is mean. Working at a club where most of the girls were on friendly terms, there was one girl who'd come in and not associate with anyone. She only worked at this place once a week and my guess is that she worked other clubs also. Everyone would try to talk to her but she just wouldn't warm up. I don't know what her problem was. Maybe she was shy, maybe she was introverted, and maybe she was just as snotty as everyone thought. This isn't the type of business where one can get away with attitude problems. This girl was good looking and had chin length brown hair with blond streaks, but wore a wig on stage. Long and blond with bangs. Nice body. When she worked at this bar she made good money. Perhaps a few of the girls were a little jealous, though certainly not all of them.

I don't have any idea what happened between the girls, but on one occasion, a feisty, slender redhead got irritated with her for something, came up behind her and pulled her wig off, on stage! The blond was mortified and most everyone was laughing, including the customers and especially the other girls working that day. They had a field day with this one.

Now I don't know if that was justified or not. Nevertheless, it was mean. Did the trick though. The wig lady left and didn't come back. Mission accomplished, I suppose.

A Foreign Phony: Superbowl Sunday. One of the clubs had a nice buffet and the money should have been pretty good. They were mostly college students working their way through school.

I was there to either pick someone up or just visit. Not sure which, it was a while ago. Anyway, all the girls were sitting around after their stage sets with very little private dancing. I asked why and they said that the tall, blond foreign girl was getting them all. She was as attractive as anyone else in there and pretended she spoke almost no English but that's not why she got all the dances. The girls said she was letting the guys touch her, lick her and play "disappearing fingers." I looked for myself. First of all, they were strict on the "no contact" rule at that time as well as keeping distance and staying on the platform. She was off the platform, directly in front of the guys, bending over and pointing to her rear, which I saw a guy lick. Right in the open!

Why didn't she get thrown out? Because the manager, who was related to the owner, was a big cocaine user. Gossip? No, he had black hair and there was always white powder on his nose hairs! Gross, I know. Found out that she'd double charge the customers for the "extras" and use the money for drugs. I GOT PISSED. Those girls were like daughters/little sisters to me and all they wanted was to buy their textbooks!

I yelled at her in front of everyone, since the manager was doing nothing, said I'd call a cop if she didn't knock it off and told her to get the f*** out. She went running to her little honey, the druggie. Next time I saw her she was telling a customer she'd have sex with him in the car for money. *I thought she didn't speak English?* OK, that's enough. I'm not getting arrested for that bimbo. I remember giving her a countdown and telling her to leave by "2" or else. Funny thing is......she was about five foot ten and I'm a peanut but she apparently got "frightened." Poor baby. The coked up manager finally got fed up with me though, grabbed my drink out of my hand and told me to leave, loudly. I laughed at him and then got irritated because he took a perfectly good drink! I took my time but eventually left.

Apparently, he straightened up, went back to his own country and married a girl from their village. See ya!

For Sale Or Rent: Once upon a time, in a little club there was a tall, very pretty brunette with long hair, green eyes and long legs to match. She was one of about six girls on that day. The club wasn't extremely crowded this Wednesday afternoon at about two o'clock. Each girl had a fifteen-minute set on stage with the rest of the time available for table dancing, changing or socializing.

On this nice day a seemingly well to do young man and his friend walked in and one of them took a liking to the pretty brunette. She went to the private area for a table dance with a smile on her face. Lo and behold, she only did one dance and then sat and talked to the man with the dark curly hair. The man ordered the girl a drink and one for his chubby friend too. When the waitress brought the drinks she saw the dark haired man hand the pretty brunette three, one hundred dollar bills and say to her, "This is for later honey."

What did the pretty girl do? Well, she didn't run away and leave behind a glass slipper. She took the money and put it away.

The story goes on. See when it was her turn to go on stage like every one else, she didn't go. No one said anything, the first time. The second time around, she didn't go on stage either. Now some of the girls were getting a little aggravated, especially one particular Italian with a hot temper and PMS that day. She wasn't able to do a table dance because she had to take the other girls turn, because the other girl was too inconsiderate to go on stage LIKE SHE WAS SUPPOSED TO! Nothing worked. The brunette must have suddenly gone deaf because she never heard anyone calling her for her turn on stage.

At the end of the shift, the brunette bolted out of the club as if she was going to turn into a pumpkin, but she DID leave something behind. A matchbook, with the phone number and hotel name that the man with the curly hair had given her. The waitress took it and…OOPS!….dropped it in the trash. When the pretty brunette came back and was looking around everywhere, the smart little waitress asked if she needed any help. Funny, the pretty brunette must have forgotten what she was looking for because she didn't need help and must have just dropped her earring somewhere else. The cute waitress and the Italian with the PMS had quite a laugh. THE END

Are You Talking to Me?: One Saturday evening, while visiting a local bar it was business as usual. An adorable blonde was dancing at the front of the stage, facing the entrance to the club and also facing a group of tables set up for customers to sit at.

One such table had three ladies sitting there. The girl on stage stopped dancing and pointed to one of the girls at the table. "So, do you still have a problem with me?" She asked. The girls at the table looked surprised. "Huh, me? Are you talking to me?" The girl answered. "Yeah, I'm talking to you! 'Do you still have a f***ing problem with me?'" That was all I heard, clearly. Before long, the little blond who couldn't have weighed more than 105 pounds was MAD. She yelled at the other girl until she got up from the table to come over for a fight.

Of course, the guys loved this. Here's a girl on stage, bare chested with her skirt up around her rear end, also bare, yelling insults and trying to start a fight on stage. *Now that I think of it, it was funny.*

The bouncer stepped in between the girls, while another bouncer stood in front of the customer. The girl on stage was so pissed off that the bouncer had to grab her and remove her from the stage, telling her she was "all done" for the night.

I wonder what really happened. I don't think the girl on stage even knew the customer! And I thought I had a temper!

One Liners—Short and sweet. These are some funny, and not so funny, things that have happened.

One girl was so lazy that she didn't want to use the bathroom. She'd pee in the sink. *Heard about it from my best friend who saw it.*

One girl was late on stage a few times because she was in the dressing room, trimming her pubic hairs with a little scissors. *Saw that one, unfortunately.*

Same girl as above, the scissors girl used to go up to the guys on stage and hold her garter out until they gave her a dollar!

More than once a dancer got so drunk she fell off the stage. *Saw that and also heard some stories.* Lots of sprained ankles.

One girl would have a few drinks and just blab and blab to anyone who'd listen, especially to the customers while they were trying to watch someone else dance. *Experienced this first hand.*

Same girl as above would have a few more drinks and blab about how she was molested as a child which is why she wouldn't get too close to the guys while on stage. *This one really needs to change professions.*

Once a girl told me she had enough cocaine for two "lines" and asked me if she should do them both now or save one for later. *What kind of a dumb question is that?*

A younger girl, early twenties, carried around a virtual pharmacy in her purse. She had prescriptions for anything and everything. Anti-inflammatory drugs, pain pills, headache pills, PMS pills, muscle relaxers and all kinds of over the counter stuff also. *She really should go into the medical profession.*

A beautiful brunette would get on stage and if she didn't see money come up right away, she'd "pout" like a kid and sit in the middle of the stage for her whole set. *I'm surprised no one gave her a pacifier!*

Another pretty girl, tall, very slim, very blond with big fake boobies, would get on stage and just smile. Aside from her physical attributes, her personality would just shine and money would come right up.

Same girl would be the "goody two shoes" and go on about how she didn't drink. Made everyone else feel like a lush until we found out she used cocaine on a regular basis. *You never know….*

Once, a girl got so smashed on her birthday that she fell off the stage and broke her arm! *Well, I'm sure this has happened way more than once.*

A girl was dancing to a sad song on stage and started to cry. Silly thing is….she picked the song! *Who'd play a slow, sad song at a strip bar anyway?*

One girl had her boyfriend break up with her in the dressing room by phone and she had to go on stage with a pretend smile on her face. Ouch!

Funny Dressing Room Stories

Gotta tell you about some of the dressing rooms and some of the stories that go along with them.

A Great Retreat: This was the best dressing room I ever saw. It was in the downstairs section of a mid-sized club. Only about six girls at a time on stage but the area was large. So was the dressing room. At the bottom of the stairs was a big curtain with a tanning bed behind it. That was awesome. They had a couple of showers with different soaps and the hottest water ever. The dressing area was huge with mirrors covering every inch of the wall above the counter. Make up lights bordered the mirrors and there were plenty of chairs, all swivel and all padded. Every few feet there were sockets for hair dryers, curling irons, etc. and there was also a pay phone downstairs so that people could make calls without hearing the noise upstairs. This was just before the time where cell phones became very popular. There was even an exit right there for those who wanted to go outside for a smoke break.

Managers would come down constantly to see that everything was okay and volunteers would come in every other day to fill baskets with condoms and literature about safe sex. Hey, why not? I haven't seen dressing rooms that nice in even some of the big expensive clubs. Loved that place. Too bad they went out of business. The town didn't want a strip bar there. Boy, you should see the other junk they have in that town! *Crack houses, car theft, car jackings, street hookers, etc.*

Is this the closet? Clubs are known to trade dancers for a night just for some new faces. Two other girls and myself went to a club about an hour and a half away to work. The place was good sized and there were quite a number of girls.

The manager showed us to the "dressing room." I thought it was the closet. This was a tiny room, barely big enough for a twin bed and one small dresser if it were a bedroom. There was only one mirror that was about three feet by three and a half feet, a small table that would have broken if something was put on it, one chair and a few lockers. The mirror was so dirty that it would have taken a bottle of cleaner to fix it.

Here's the funny part. We were changing when in walks one of the "house girls" who danced there on a regular basis. A busty bleached blond with a big, bubbly personality to match her boobs. She unlocked her locker, took out a little backpack, looked at us and asked if anyone wanted to buy tranquilizers or painkillers. Cracked me up. She had no idea who we were. We could have been the police, but she didn't care. Very amusing.

The rest of the evening was interesting. It took most of the evening for the house girls to warm up to us. About an hour before closing some of them got a little too warm. They were hitting on us, in front of everyone, on stage. Many were pretty drunk by this time and it was no act. The guys sure liked it.

We ended up making pretty good money and staying till closing. Tired, getting in at about 3:30 am. We all laughed about the drug sales lady.

Come Into My Office…..Just Past All the Naked Girls: In a small bar, the dressing room was in the back of the club. It was also in the path that lead to the mens room and when the door opened it opened on all the girls. As you might guess, some guys would try to walk by slowly to sneak a peek. Even though it was a bar with total nudity, I guess there's something about watching the girls get ready.

What drove us nuts though was that the owners office was in there also, just past the door to the dressing room, to the right. It made sense to have it near the dressing room so he could talk to the girls easily about scheduling, etc., but it was just TOO close. Whenever he'd bring anyone in to his office, they had to go through the dressing room….and they loved it. Some of the characters he'd bring back there honestly didn't deserve special treatment. I'd always wear something back there like a robe, long shirt, etc. and change "under" things. No one could get a free peek, including the grabby owner!

The Super Polite Manager: Small club. The bartender, would come downstairs to the dressing room to let girls know they were on next or tell them they were late, etc. This guy was so polite that he'd knock on the door and wouldn't enter the room till someone opened the door. Funny thing is what he'd say, Knock knock…."Are you girls decent?" It's a dressing room for nude dancers. How much clothing did he think we had on anyway? Nevertheless, it was kinda cute, (so was he).

A MYTH: These bars are terrible, dangerous places to work in. Sure, a woman can run into a psychopath or stalker, but that can happen anywhere. It's a controlled atmosphere.—I've had guys grab me in places they shouldn't at regular bars, not strip bars. No one in his or her right or sober mind would try that in a strip bar. They don't call them "gentlemen's clubs" for nothing, you know! Behave like gentlemen or get tossed out.

I left this end of the business for various reasons. Obvious one would be my age, but not the main one. I could have worked in management, bartending, etc., but would honestly get "burned out" quickly. Many if not all dancers experience burn out, where they just have to get away for a while. Lots of reasons for this. For me I have to say it was the girls that stressed me out and for good reason. Being twice everyone else's age, I'd see things differently. Too many stressed out kids who didn't belong there; too many kids blowing their money up their noses and too many screwed up stories. This isn't everyone's story, but that's how it went for me.

THE PRIVATE WORLD:
PRIVATE ONE ON ONE DANCING

Private dancing. We've seen in movies, heard songs about it and have had all sorts of mixed thoughts about the subject. Does anyone ever really hire a woman to come to his place and dance? Yes they do. For various reasons some gentlemen prefer to have a one-on-one show for just them. It will surely cost more than being in a bar, but the client gets to make choices. He can request a certain type of outfit, music, theme, etc., in the comfort and privacy of his own home. Here's how I ended up doing this type of work.

What was originally planned as a cleaning service turned into something a bit different. I decided to start a "French Maid Cleaning Service." Sure, it's been done, plenty of times, but there was nothing like that in our area so I thought I'd try it. The idea was simple. A woman, probably me at first, would go to the home or place of business, change into a sexy French Maid costume and actually clean. His beverage would be poured, his pillow on his favorite chair fluffed and his place cleaned, all for only $35 an hour. He'd be allowed to follow into each room being cleaned to observe the sexy outfit. Fun. Great gift idea for any occasion. Didn't go quite as I'd planed. Had some calls, did some cleaning jobs and met some nice guys, but they all wanted more.

They were happy with the cleaning but would do without it for more nudity. I decided to up the price to $75 an hour for forty-five minutes of cleaning and fifteen minutes of stripping to the undies. That worked, but boys will be boys, and they didn't really care about the cleaning at all. They wanted the nudity and the dancing. I found that many preferred not to go to the strip bars because of their professions or marital status, so I'd bring the strip bar to them. It would be completely discrete and private.

They could be the principals of a school or a married lawyer and no one would know. After all, what would be the harm? They just wanted some entertainment. *The men who wanted "more" were told to call an escort service.* Men are funny…They didn't want to pay $35 an hour for a sexy cleaning lady, but would gladly pay $125 for a one-hour private dancer! Now isn't that a surprise!

So, I hired a bodyguard to go with me and got all the information from the client that I'd need to be safe. A cross-reference of their phone number insured that they were who they said they were. Clients were informed ahead of time that someone would be very close by and would be calling their home phone at various intervals.

If that was OK, I'd go in, check their id and change into a sexy outfit. While changing, I'd observe the surroundings and make comments on things, especially photos. "Oh, are these your kids?" I'd also ask them which car was theirs for directional purposes. Really, I'd take the plate number down. Now I'd know a lot about the client. I don't think it's ever truly safe, but then again, what is?

How did I keep someone entertained for an hour? Easy. A few minutes for an intro, another few for an id check, chitchat, changing, more chit chat, preparing music, dancing, more chit chat, changing and a good bye. My bodyguard would call after the first five minutes initially, then every fifteen. He'd call them by first name and ask for me. We had code words in case of a problem, but fortunately, there was never a need for anything drastic. Most guys I met were nice, just looking for some entertainment as I said before.

Following are some of my clients:

*College professor who was married and didn't want to be seen at a strip bar.

*Dean at a college…..same reason.

*An attorney. He was single and could go to the bars, but liked the one on one attention. He loved to talk and couldn't do that in a strip club where there are so many distractions. He was really nice. Wonder what happened to him?

*Owner of several of good sized local businesses. He had a "good boy" reputation with a "good girl" for a girlfriend. Didn't want to ruin it by letting his family know that he enjoyed the art of the striptease. I'd bet money that the "goody" girlfriend acts like a total wild woman at an all-male review! Those are usually the ones.

*Married guy, in the pro sports field, who liked the rush of having a dancer over a half hour after his wife went to work! She worked night shift and didn't start till 11:00. He'd put the kids to bed and call me! I'd flip out if that was my guy, but I was there to entertain, not judge.

*Single guy, 50, in the banking field who wouldn't go to bars because of his past alcohol addiction.

*Single guy, 40, who was looking for a girlfriend! Wanted to take me to dinner more than have me dance for him. I realized that he was a drug user and I'm not talking about a little pot. He was well behaved but the drugs were too much. He went to the bathroom more times than a pregnant woman and wiped his nose more than I do on my worst allergy days! *I stopped dancing for him because of that.*

*Note: You never know why things happen. One of the above guys has become one of my best friends. He's the sweetest, most loyal friend I've ever met and we've been close for years now (Not the druggie) so, something really nice came out of all that crazy work.

There were a few odd stories. Here's a real good one. Probably the most dangerous situation I've found myself in while doing this crazy job and I must admit it did give me the creeps. I also gave this aspect of the entertainment business up after this incident.

The Man With the White Latex Gloves

I was about 10 miles from my home, only two towns over in a decent neighborhood with two and three story homes, yards, fences, kids, etc., an average area. When the gentleman we'll call "Sam" first called, I explained my services. I explained as usual that any type of sex or sexual contact was not on the program, which he was fine with. Sam said he was a single man in his 40's who was a bit on the lonely side and didn't like the strip bar scene as he'd given up alcohol and wasn't comfortable there anymore. He also said he thought it was impersonal. I spoke with him about a half an hour on the phone before I accepted the appointment to dance for him. We had a nice, friendly chat and I agreed to see him.

As usual, I took a bodyguard with me who I referred to as my "driver" to the clients. That wasn't a lie. He was the driver. Also there to protect me if need be. I was dropped off and after five minutes, received my first phone call to make sure that initially all was okay. All was fine. The driver would call me back in fifteen.

"Sam" was well groomed, wearing shorts and a T-shirt, bare feet, glasses and a military buzz cut hairstyle. He said he was over forty. He was trim, neat, polite and friendly, although, not bubbly. I entered the place. He politely pointed me to the bathroom where I changed. He was pleased with the outfit and my appearance in general. I recall wearing a tiny, tight short dress with a snow leopard print. It had little straps and a flared hem that moved when I did. Underneath, I wore a black lace bra, matching G-string, black, lace top thigh highs and very high heels. Sam put some music on. Phil Collins I believe. I'd have no problem dancing to this.

He sat comfortably on a big chair and I began to dance for him. I did my routine and near the end, when I was about to change back to my regular clothing, he asked for a "little more." I sounded insulted and he immediately apologized. Said he just "liked" me, no insult intended. No problem. I collected my fee. I think he felt guilty because he gave me a nice tip. Maybe, he'd be a regular client. At least till he found himself a girlfriend.

During the next couple of weeks, he'd call just to chat for a few. He'd call a pager and I'd call him back. I've become friends with some clients and occasionally gave out my home number, but instinct said not to this time. Keep it friendly, but business, not friendship. Boy, was I right on target. When someone tells you to trust your instincts, they mean it. Here's what happened.

He called, saying he'd received a bonus check from work and wanted to hire me again. Okay. When I arrived, he stopped me in the stair well and said his roommate was home also. "Would you prefer I leave and come back another time?" I asked. "No" he replied. "But I wish you didn't have a driver. See, I told my roommate all about you." OK, I get it. He thinks we're dating. I was right. Sam was slightly embarrassed. "Uh…yeah…" he said with his eyes toward the floor. "And your driver, well, he'll call and it will sound like business and." "Don't worry about it," I replied. "I'll take care of everything."

I gave him a pat on the shoulder for comfort and we went upstairs to his third floor apartment. There, sat a middle-aged gentleman, well in his 40's with thinning hair and a comfortable tummy. He was stretched out on his sofa, watching TV when I entered the room and sat down. Stanley was pleasant and friendly and happy to talk about his love for music, pointing out his massive CD collection as well as his passion for painting. His paintings were all over the place. Scenery mostly. His were watercolors while I paint in oils so we had something to talk about. After about fifteen minutes of chat, Sam retreated to his bedroom, inviting me in. I thanked Stanley for his hospitality, the place was actually his, remarked on his artwork and excused myself to go and be with my "date".

I shut the door to the bedroom, which was right next to the den that Stanley was in so I'm sure he could hear us talk. I "giggled" like a girl. I'm sure Stanley thought that this was one booming romance. That's exactly what he was supposed to think. Sam looked happy. While I put my purse down and prepared to begin a dance, Sam relaxed on his bed.

After the music started, Sam did something REALLY ODD. He reached over to a night table and picked up white latex gloves, the medical kind. You know, the kind doctors wear, the kind that cops wear, the kind that a coroner would wear, the kind a killer would wear! His eyes were moving about the room and gazing at nothing. A red flag went up. Hmmmm. what do I do here. I just told my driver five minutes ago that all was just fine and that he could call back in twenty-five minutes!

I told Stanley, the roommate, that the call was from my brother who borrowed the car and would be picking me up later. Well, I guess I was on my own. Let's see how much psychology I really knew.

"Sam …Uh, why are you wearing gloves?" I asked simply. He really looked dazed and answered; "I'm going to give you the white glove treatment tonight." OK, I thought. He's looking for dust? I asked him what that meant. He responded that his "hands were rough from working with toxic chemicals on the job." Oh, now that's what I really wanted to hear. Here's some guy that just snapped into the twilight zone and I find out he works with toxic chemicals. And just what did these chemicals do to his brain, I wonder? So I said, "Well, it's OK. You don't have to touch me you know." He just repeated his "white glove" comment. Now what? Here's an idea. Just hear this one out before you make a judgment.

Now remember, I know that Stanley is just outside and hoped he'd help if I SCREAMED. But he could be just as nuts! "Here sweetie. Take off your shirt and relax. Lie down on your bed and I'll rub your back for you. You look a little tense and stressed." He just did what I said. No questions asked. *I did have a plan…you know.*

I spoke softly to him, put lotion on his back and adjusted a pillow for his head. I told him not to move his head from side to side because his muscles were tense, and to put his face down into the soft pillow. I also told him to put his hands under the pillow. He did. With him in this position I began snooping, with my eyes. I noticed a prescription bottle on his dresser. I asked him if he was OK. He said yes. I told him I'd noticed medicine and wondered if he'd been sick. He said, "No, they're to help me sleep." I asked why he had trouble sleeping. Moving his head slightly he said, still with the glazed over eyes, "Well, I have these bad dreams." He went on to say that his dreams were because of things that happened to him in the war. He said he wasn't proud of the things he'd done there. I didn't ask what they were. I just thought to myself, "Oh great, here's some poor guy, all messed from that stupid war and he's gonna take it out on me. I probably remind him of his mean mother or something."

I moved back and just asked, "OK, are you going to kill me, cut me in pieces and feed me to the neighbor's dog or something?" "No" was his simple answer. "Then would you PLEASE lose those gloves? They're really making me nervous." He took them off and I breathed a sigh of relief…sort of. I sat on the floor again and softly told him that it's okay to mess up. We all do and need to forgive ourselves make our lives better and move on. He responded and calmed down. His eyes returned to the planet and he began talking about music again. I really felt like a shrink. Guess I had to be in this situation. I continued to talk to him, asking about the good things he'd done in his life so far and assured him there would be lots more.

The phone FINALLY rang. It was my driver, downstairs, waiting for me. Boy, that was a long twenty five minutes! I gathered my things, still talking about the nice things in life, left the room, said goodnight to his roommate and flew downstairs. He handed me my fee, even though I didn't really dance. I took it and ran.

It was such a weird experience. Made me realize how dangerous it is to be with strangers even if you think you know them. With age/wisdom/maturity on my side, I was able to handle this. I had to be the one in control without letting him know I even had the control. Psychoanalyze him and figure out the best plan, all at one time. It worked. So ladies, even if you're not a private dancer, DON'T go to a guy's place unless you REALLY know him!

Sam called again a couple of weeks later to thank me for helping and to let me know he'd never have me over again as a dancer. *Like I'd be going back anyway?* He said he felt it was "wrong". He also confessed that at the time I worked for him, he'd slipped back into some "old bad habits," one being cocaine. He didn't show what I'd think of as typical signs of the drug, but then again, you've read my stories on that subject. Well, maybe this would account for some of his irrational behavior. He never called again. Of course, I tossed the pager. I hope I never run into him again and if I do, maybe he won't recognize me. I've gone from very black hair to very blond! To Mr. Gloves: I hope your life is back on track and you're sleeping well.

Mistaken Identity: A very good friend called and asked me to dance for one of his business associates. I'd met the associate before, had socialized with him and figured it would be okay. All set.

The associate called to ask if his business partner could join him. Generally I'd say no, but since I knew this guy, I agreed. My friend was one of their best clients and they had a lot of respect for him. They wouldn't want to lose his business.

I got there and was greeted by the associate that I knew. He was friendly and courteous. I had a bodyguard with me who saw me to the door, said he'd be downstairs at a little bar, shook hands with the associate and left. Now I met the partner. What a difference! They weren't at all alike. He was crude, rude, irritable, jumpy and had absolutely NO CLASS.

I'd been asked ahead of time to join them at a restaurant and the partner got upset with me because I didn't know directions to the establishment. We were out of town at a convention. How the heck would I know the local restaurants? To top that off, he asked if my driver was a pimp and if I'd ever had two guys sexually at the same time. By this time, I'm thinking that he's not funny at all. Still not knowing if he was just kidding, I simply answered, "No." He said he found that hard to believe.

He got worse. He asked me for condoms. I simply said that I don't carry condoms. He was actually annoyed! By this time I wanted to belt him. Turns out he thought I was someone else, a girl from the town where we were who was a dancer by day, and an escort by evening. It made more sense now although it didn't excuse his nasty behavior. He even stopped at a little convenience store with me right there and said, loudly and laughing, "Do you sell condoms?" He also was speaking in a different language to his partner. That's OK though, I got him back.

We went out for food first and the partner was just plain obnoxious. On top of that, he smoked some pot, which made him act even more stupid. He was still rude, just laughing a lot. When it was time to dance for them, he made a few more smart-ass comments. The original client told him he should apologize to me. I said, holding my tongue, "no problem," thinking he'd stop if I was "nice." Well that didn't work. When he made some totally disrespectful comment concerning my family member whom he didn't even know, he'd gone over the edge. I stopped dancing, stopped the music and said: "NOW, you owe me an apology. How'd you like me to make rude comments about your family?" He said he wouldn't like that.

I asked him if he thought I was sweet, soft spoken and gentle, in a nice voice, and he said yes. Then I raised my voice and said, "You think you're tough because you're an *!#$" (don't want to mention his nationality). He nodded his proud head. "Well, I'm Italian and you DON'T want to rile my temper now do you? Trust me, you don't want to see me mad." I have no idea what he expected but he humbly apologized and was a "good boy" the rest of the evening. What did he think I'd do? Throw salami at him? I also analyzed his handwriting and the guy was freaked. I didn't hold anything back. Well, he deserved more, but I'll never see him again so who cares?

My Wife Doesn't Mind: I received a call from a man in response to the sexy house cleaning/dancing ad. He, like 95% of the others, wasn't interested in house cleaning. He was interested in the dancing. After talking to him for half an hour and collecting the proper information, I made an appointment with him.

He showed me the proper identification, etc. and made himself comfortable on the sofa. He was friendly, cheery, and playful and we immediately got along on friendly terms as opposed to only business. Sometimes people just click. He wanted to have fun and had all of his money changed into one-dollar bills! As I danced, he threw money and when I was sure he really was a gentleman, I let him stuff them in my stockings and garter. He remained perfectly well behaved; we had a few laughs and just talked for the remaining half-hour. He told me that his wife knew where he was, what he was doing and that he wanted me to meet her. Huh? I didn't believe him so he called her, put me on the phone to say hello and told her he was being a good boy.

The next couple of times he hired me, his wife was there too! She was shy and uncomfortable the first time but by the second time she liked it too. They wanted to "spice things up" a bit and it appeared to be working. The three of us became friends. Personally, I don't think I'd have handled it as well as she did, but they'd been married over twenty years and were very secure with each other. Since they both agreed, why not?

After a while, he'd buy me outfits to wear for dancing, get us both flowers and champagne, light the room with candles and even bring munchies 'cause he knew I liked them! Such a romantic. *He treated his wife like this all the time, by the way.* I'd even go Christmas shopping with the husband for the wife. We had such fun in the lingerie stores, would go to lunch, then call her and tell her we got her presents! These were nice honest people, which are not so easy to find these days. In case you're wondering, it wasn't a sexual thing. Sexy, yes, sexual, no.

Let's Dress Him Up: Another couple. Two more nice people who I danced for a few times. The second or third time I danced for them, the husband had something different in mind. He wanted to dance for us! Fine by me.

We poured ourselves some white wine and waited to be entertained. When he started to undress he had on a pair of beautiful, black, beaded bikinis. All I heard was, "So you've got my panties! I've been looking all over for them!" Thought I'd crack up laughing.

It turned out he liked to wear women's undies on occasion and this was one of them. He'd taken his wife's most expensive pair of black velvet panties. His fantasy was for us dress him up and have him dance for us. So we did, including stockings, bra, makeup, the whole works. He even brought two lipsticks and let us decide which one would look best. We put on some music and he did a nice strip tease for us.

It was an interesting evening with a couple of fun people and I got paid to top it off. This was the good side of the private world. When I decided to end this phase of the business I thought it was because of the dangers, but in looking back, it wasn't. I simply got tired of the 70% of the guys that would continuously ask for "more." When that wasn't an option, some would ask for dates or a relationship. When that wasn't an option, they'd stop calling and/or not want to deal with me at all.

Bachelor Parties/Stags:

Those dreaded words that no woman enjoys hearing. A bachelor party. Are they really as wild as you hear? Do the girls get completely naked and let the guy lick whipped cream off of their bodies? Do they bump and grind the bachelor or just strip for him? Does anyone pop out of a cake anymore? How about those "girl on girl" shows? Just what do the two girls do with each other? The most frightful question, do the girls give the guys anything "extra" for a price?

This is a tough section to write about if I want to be honest, but I said I would be so I will. All those terrible stories you hear about bachelor parties are not always a lie. Yes, those wild bachelor parties do happen with all kinds of crazy things going on, but most certainly not all the time. Like with any other party, some are mild and some are not.

Now before any of us get judgmental, let's think about it for a moment. There's a guy getting married. He's made it known publicly that he's devoting himself to one woman for the rest of his life, proving his love for her by declaring his faithfulness in front of God and family. Someone gives him a bachelor party. A farewell to the single life, which he's technically given up already by having a fiancé. There's food, gifts for a raffle, music, lots of alcohol, maybe some gambling and an entertainer.

Now even if she is one of the wilder women and offers to give the groom to be more than a dance, who's fault is it if he accepts? Shouldn't he be strong enough to say no? Shouldn't he want to say no? If it were me and the guy didn't have enough will power to resist another woman before the wedding, what would make me think he'd be faithful after the wedding? Common sense would answer that one.

I'll tell you about some of the parties I've been to, danced at and heard of.

The Bodyguard: First of all, the girls do take someone with them. A bodyguard/driver. While one guy couldn't control an entire crowd, no matter how large his build, he can watch over things. The guy I took with me all the time would drive me to the place, go in ahead of me to check out the situation and if all was OK and the fee was paid, I'd go in. He would hold on to the money, stand by the door while I got ready, put the music on and just watch. Watch the guys to make sure they were behaving and watch them to see if anyone was about to fight. Should a fight begin to break out, it was his job to get the dancer (me in this case) safely out of the way and out of the place. This guy was exceptional. He'd observe the crowd, take care of the music, hold the money, fold it all face up and even make change for the guys. He was remarkable. To my bodyguard: THANK YOU!

Size of the Parties: Varied. Some were small and in homes and others were large and in halls. The smallest party I danced at was probably for six guys and the largest was for about 125, with just one dancer. Homes, halls, a hotel suite, backyards and even a bus!

Many times more than one girl would be hired. It could be a two-girl act where both look and dress alike, or are totally different. Sometimes, more than one girl is hired to entertain at different times. Depends on what the guys want.

I like to include "strip-o-grams" in this section. Could be a birthday surprise, someone leaving a company, moving, etc. Whatever the reason, they're usually funny, especially for the guy who's being surprised. The strip-o-gram takes much less time than a party, lasting around twenty minutes or so, or about three or four songs. Many times you'll see the cop uniform or the nurses outfit, pizza delivery person, etc. for these occasions. They're short and sweet. You're in and out of there.

The Parties

Here are first hand accounts of a handful of parties I've worked. Some were really crazy and others were subdued. Tell you the truth, the ones that were too mild were actually more work because the guys weren't easily entertained.

First Party: Oh, what a way to get initiated into this line of the business. I was working at a bar in my area, when I ran into another dancer I hadn't seen in a while. She was a waitress with me back at that first little club. Since then, we'd both switched to dancing. We always got along and she mentioned that she was working a bachelor party the coming weekend. Her original partner couldn't make it and she asked if I'd fill in. She assured me that I'd be picked up by her and a bodyguard, we'd be paid well and our tips were our own. What the heck. I liked and trusted her, I needed the money and it sounded like fun.

Saturday night came and I was picked up on time. We traveled about 45 minutes from my place and got to a hall just full of guys. There had to be over a hundred. We changed and were immediately given shots and drinks. A "White Russian" and a "Carrot Cake" if I remember correctly. I didn't know that a shot tasting like carrot cake was so strong and their idea of a white Russian was not white but brown. They used about two drops of milk.

Being a super lightweight in the alcohol department, combined with absolutely no knowledge of the stuff, I had no idea how it can hit you so quickly.

*Note: If I haven't mentioned it already, I HONESTLY never had a drink till I was over forty. No weird reasons, just had a bad experience, only one, as a teen with some cough syrup full of alcohol and it literally left a bad taste in my mouth. Long story. *Let's just say that the sixteen-year-old boy who told me to drink it was really cute and I was being a dumb kid.* It just lasted twenty-five years! So I was a real newcomer to the drinking scene.

Anyway, the other girl told me to just start dancing and she would lead. She said we'd be working topless only. The music started, we start moving, she reaches for something and turns around, spraying whipped cream right in between my boobs! Surprise! Then proceeds to lick it off. She did this quickly and made it look sexier than it was but I didn't know that was coming. We then went from guy to guy, dancing together and separately for tips, plus we were paid.

The drinks kept coming and the guys were pretty rowdy, yet not out of control. There were no problems. We got so many "thank you's" and compliments and the money was really fantastic.

What did I learn from this? Those bachelor parties can yield a lot of quick cash for a few hours of work, including the traveling and preparing. I also learned to limit the alcohol. Just say "no thank you" and if I was going to drink at all, don't let anyone try to bench press me like one big guy tried to do. It's too much contact and makes you dizzy! Also, I never let anyone I worked with take the lead again, not knowing what to expect. I took the lead from that time on and planned things differently. And if I want to be totally honest, she was using cocaine in the dressing room.

Working alone: When the girl in the first story parted from the agency, the agent began calling me every weekend for parties. Most of them were in the next state and the traveling would be anywhere from forty five minutes to two hours. The agent tried to make sure that the parties were good ones if I had to travel that far, plus he'd throw in a little extra for traveling expenses. Basically, he just booked the parties and made money for it. All you need is an entertainment license and advertisement. Of course he also got all the headaches if someone didn't show up or if the girl wasn't what they expected, showed up smashed or so stoned that she couldn't walk, etc. He also had to hear from the girls if the parties weren't good, the customers got out of hand, didn't tip well, etc. So, he can have the aggravation. I'd rather do the work.

I began to put my own tapes together as well as costume ideas. I'd ask questions about the bachelor or birthday guy. Age, race, likes and dislikes. Does he like R & B, rock, garters and stockings, any fantasies? That way I could put together something just for him.

Most of the guys getting married were between twenty-two, the youngest, and thirty-nine or so. I don't remember many over forty. Here are some I do remember:

How About Some Vanilla with the Chocolate? This party is the reason I started asking more details about the party hosts.

I arrived at a house party on a warm June evening. There were girls partying on the second floor and guys on the third. Seemed like a nice crowd. Only thing a little weird, I was pretty much the only Caucasian person there. I think that in a crowd of twenty-five guys there might have been one other white person.

I have nothing against being the only different one but I hoped they'd like me. Fortunately, we all got along very well. They just didn't like my choice of music so I had them put on something they preferred. I was into sensual rock at the time and they liked dance and R&B. Everything worked out just fine and by the second song, guys were dancing with me and everyone had fun.

One Other Time: My friend and I had a large bachelor party to work, about two hours away. It was still very warm when we arrived in the area, so people were lounging outside in their yards, on the doorsteps, kids playing, etc. We heard talking but couldn't understand anyone. It didn't seem like anybody was speaking English. That's because they weren't. We heard music from passing cars and from open windows. It wasn't English either.

We entered the house after the bodyguard spoke to the guy in charge and most of them didn't speak English. Fortunately, no one cared what we spoke, as long as they saw naked girls dance and whatever music we played was fine with them. I guess a sexy woman translates the same in all languages.

The Pharmacy Student: This party was for a guy graduating from pharmacy school. Since it was medical, I thought it would be fun to dress like a naughty nurse. You know, all white with garters, stockings and the whole bit.

The gathering was at a private home and I remember it was a scorching hot night in July and very humid. There were about twenty guys all totaled, on the younger side, some friendly, some a little shy who all warmed up after a few drinks.

I brought along some props, which helped make it really fun. A stethoscope, some little candies that I gave them for "medicine" and a couple of little squirt guns which I filled with whiskey and vodka to give them their "shots." It went well, though the money could have been a little better. Like I said, these guys were pretty young. By the end of the party I filled the squirt guns with ice water and let them squirt me! Hey, I'm no dummy…it was hot as heck and they couldn't open doors or shades because of the neighbors. Went out for a nice cold beer afterward with the bodyguard.

The Fire Station: This one was fun. Due to the large amount of guys, they needed two girls. We'd known each other before so it was easy to work together. She was the shy one out of the two of us so I usually took the lead. At the time, I was a brunette and she was blonde. I'd usually tan darker on purpose and we made a nice contrast.

We had to drive quite a distance for this one, close to two hours. Fortunately, there were plenty of firemen and their friends there. The poor bodyguard had just undergone surgery on his knee only a few days before and was in some serious pain but he was a trooper and took us anyway.

The party was actually held upstairs in the fire station, which was kind of fun, except for the injured bodyguard climbing stairs. The other girl and myself went downstairs and got the hats and coats of the bachelor and best man, put them on and waddled upstairs. Those outfits are heavy! How they put fires out wearing them is beyond me. We entered the room and announced the numbers on the hats, asking the owners to come and claim their belongings. When the two guys eagerly came up and the whole crowd started "hooting and hollering" we knew this was going to be a good night. It was.

From the start, the guys were on the rowdy side. Our first sign of that was when the groom and best man got their hats and the remaining bridal party gave us rulers to spank the guys. The thing is, they willingly bent over, and wanted us to smack their bare bottoms. Time to take over here. I announced that we didn't want to see any bare rear ends unless they were ours and that all the "boys" here needed to keep their drawers on. They listened. More of a threat than any bodyguard is the idea of the dancers walking out.

After we danced for the bridal party and started to go around to everyone else, the guys were hovering and crowding us, making it difficult for our bodyguard to see. One guy kept getting grabby and we didn't want him to spoil it for everyone, including us. *By this time, the drinking had increased by a large degree.*

We asked for room and instead, went table to table, dancing for each other, being very sexy. The guys loved it and kept throwing us money. The bodyguard would simply go to each table, telling everyone at the other table to stay put until we got there. They were pretty good, we didn't get bothered and everyone had a good time, plus we made some really incredible money that night. By the way, we did give those two boys a good spanking….no bare bottoms, but I'm sure those rulers to the boxer shorts stung.

Live & Learn: Before I had the greatest bodyguard I had the worst. A guy who I'd become acquainted with in my area offered to help work a bachelor party with me. I knew I'd need someone to go with me and I thought he'd be OK. Although he wasn't large in stature, I knew that's not what mattered, as long as he paid attention and kept his eyes on the crowd. At the time, he was also extremely infatuated with a friend of mine. One party in particular was near her house. He suggested we pick her up afterwards and go for drinks. I remember that the party was small and he rushed me through it so he could have more time with my friend. I also noticed that he was drinking a lot more than he should have while he was working. I'm no expert, but I thought his judgment might be a little clouded by all that booze.

I brushed it off as nerves on his part as he was unsure how the lady felt about him. I knew things with him were off but I was concentrating on what I was doing. What I didn't know was that he was a thief and a total drunk. It took me a few shows to find out for sure.

At one party, he asked, more like begged my friend to come along and keep him company. *Like he needed company while he was supposed to be working.* She came along, which was fine with me and all night he kept going back and forth to the bar, buying them both drinks and overly tipping the bartender. (For stronger drinks, I presume) What she and I didn't know was that he was using MY money. He made up a story that someone at the party must have "stolen" a hundred-dollar bill, which is why I was short. Actually I was short much more but took his word…dummy me. Besides, wasn't it his job to protect the money?

Instinct had told me from the start that he was not right, but I just didn't want to believe it. Truthfully, it was easier to fool myself than face a confrontation. He seemed like such a nice young man. I also had no concrete proof. Tough situation. Here was this guy, trying to impress my girlfriend and at that point she was starting to like him. If he was stealing, I certainly didn't want her around him and if he wasn't, it looked like an idiot. So, I waited.

The Jerk Kept Stealing: At my third party, the place was jumping, the crowd was large and the tips were great. Guys were stuffing $20's and $10's in my garter for what would usually be a one or two dollar dance. I'd collect a bunch of money and bring it to the bodyguard to sort and hold, going back and forth many times. He held it all right, in his pocket. This was another night that my girlfriend came along. The crowd of guy liked my pretty friend and wanted her to strip. The girl never danced a day in her life but had enough cocktails in her to get a little gutsy. (Thanks to the thieving bodyguard)

Holidays were approaching and some extra cash would be nice so I took her by the hand out to the middle of the floor where she took her sweater off. They were thrilled with the bra and started giving her money! I told her to take it for what it was worth and try something. She danced for a couple of guys. More money. Now they asked for the bra to come off. She was hesitant but when they started handing her five's and tens she lost her shyness. That was about it. She danced around a little in her jeans with no top and made some quick pocket money for the holidays. Incidentally, this is what got her into the business.

I was having so much fun with her that I never noticed the stupid "bodyguard" spending more time at the bar than watching us. When we left and I counted the money, I knew for sure something was wrong. There were far too many twenties for there to be so little money. He said he cashed them in at the bar. OK, then there should have been hundred dollar bills. He had no answers or excuses.

The three of us went back to my house afterward and he was so drunk he passed out dead on my couch. I told my friend about the theft and why I'd waited to say anything. She understood and fortunately took my word for it. We looked through his pockets but found nothing. The idiot not only stole but also spent it all at the bar. She stopped hanging around with the loser.

I confronted him. He denied everything and I cut my losses. I knew I'd never get the money back. Turns out I was right. Found out months later that he ended up in jail for breaking and entering, his own house no less. How pathetic. Like I said at the beginning....Live & Learn.

Diana Saves The Day: This is actually part of the story above. At this large party, a guy was videotaping, without permission. I noticed it and asked him to stop. He didn't. Just kept filming. I TOLD him to stop. He didn't. I covered up and went to the bodyguard, the thief. He was halfway smashed by now and gave a sorry attempt to talk the guy into giving the tape over. By this time the recorder was shut. Not good enough. I wanted the tape. I had no idea how much he'd filmed and as my "bodyguard" wasn't paying attention, he had no idea either.

Diana (the name of the friend I keep referring to) got sick of the whole thing, went up to the guy and literally grabbed the video camera out of his hand. She opened it, took out the tape, tore it up and gave him back the camera. She looked at all of us and just said, "There!" What was the guy going to do? Hit her? I don't think so. He behaved the rest of the evening. I owe her big time for that one, considering that the guy wasn't filming her, just me at the time and she just stood up to him. Thanks honey!

We Can Fake It: I figure there's a way around everything. Got a call from the agent to do a smaller bachelor party. No problem. He asked if Diana would join me. I told him that she'd been thinking about it and I might be able to talk her into it. I did. I told her it was a small party with about fifteen guys and we'd be just fine. She agreed.

Arrangements were made. "By the way," he said, you do know that this is a "girl on girl show, don't you?" Uh....sure, I guess. "What the hell is that, I'm thinking?" Oh....I get it. They want girl interaction. Hmmm......So that's why the price on this one was up even though it wasn't too far away. Without hesitation (or thinking) I said OK. Oh great, now I have to tell Diana, who I had to talked into this, that she has to make this look real. I suggested that we get together to practice dancing, just close enough to be very seductive, brush our hair over each other, play with the clothes, etc., nothing more. We can fake it! She was okay with that.

The party was at a private home and we realized that there would be little room between us girls and the guys, let alone a stage to perform on. The guys weren't terribly drunk and to top it off, five of them were doctors. They pointed some spotlights at us and waited for us to get ready. When asked if we needed anything, I never heard Diana speak up so fast. "A beer and a shot....now!" Turned out okay. We won them over with our personalities and entertaining skills and let them know that, although we have nothing against girls with girls, our act was just an act. When they asked for more interactions, we told them it was a classy show for classy guys. *Fast thinking, huh?* They liked that; we made money and left happy.

I thought Diana was going to kill me! This is how all the rest of the parties we did together went. We'd get into some sort of mess and I'd try to smooth everything over. The reasons we got into half the messes were usually my bright ideas anyway! Poor girl....it's amazing she still talks to me!

Dance For Grandpa: At a relatively large party, I was given a $20 to go over and dance for grandpa. There sat this little eighty-four year old guy, bald, glasses, just as cute as can be with a big smile on his face. In nothing but a bra and panty I sat right on his knee and gave him a kiss on the cheek along with rubbing his little bald head. He seemed so harmless. All the young guys around him were cheering and just as I was about to get up....he grabbed my boobs! How "cute" was he now? Oh well, the guy was eighty-four and got a cheap thrill. I wonder if they told grandma what he did. Probably not. *I didn't dance for him again....the dirty boy!*

The Moving Bus: Believe it or not, I danced on a chartered bus while it was moving. It was a bachelor party with about twenty guys. They hired a bus to take everyone to a casino, planned to stay a couple of hours and come home. My job was to dance on the way down and a little on the way back. I'm a little nutty, so I said I'd do it. On this occasion, my agent was along for the ride, so I didn't want to mess up. Pretty hard not to mess up while dancing on a moving vehicle I'd later find out.

I changed into a costume in a tiny little bathroom on the bus. Not only was it a physical challenge but I had to rush due to the guys waiting for the bathroom. Those who'd already had a few beers couldn't exactly "go outside." The rest of the bus was large enough, with seats, couches and tables and a fully stocked bar.

Before I began to dance, everyone was given a plastic cup full of some sort of shot to toast the groom. I asked what it was and they said it was peach schnapps. "Are you sure?" I questioned. "Yes." they replied. Guess the joke was on me when we toasted. "Drink it all at once," they insisted. OK, I'll be a sport I thought. Guess what? It wasn't peach. It was tequila! Never knew my throat could burn like that! Could have killed those brats. Even more so when the stuff kicked in about ten minutes later. Try to dance now, I remind you, on a moving bus. Well, fortunately, I'd eaten dinner so it didn't hit me too badly.

We got to the casino and I dressed really nice, wearing a black velvet dress, heels, long gloves, a pearl bracelet and necklace. Very classy. Walked in with two gents on each arm and two right behind me. The rest followed. It was fun. People were looking, which is what they wanted. I can imagine some were thinking, "Who's that? An actress?" and others, "What the hell are they trying to do?" After we got inside everyone went his own way to gamble a bit and meet again on the bus. I put another outfit on and danced for about twenty minutes on the way back. The money wasn't spectacular, but it was good and it sure was an experience. After that I never touched tequila…yuck.

The Birthday Boy: I do mean boy. I was hired for a birthday party, told where to go and who to see. The contact person was a woman, hiring a dancer for a birthday party. Now it's usually for someone's big forty or something like that. Not this one.

I got to the door, with the bodyguard by my side and a nice woman, probably in her forties met us at the door. She paid the fee and told us the party was being held outside. She assured me that the high fence made the yard private. There was a mixed crowd, men and women and some younger kids. The rules: No younger people outside and no public nudity. This would be more like a bikini show. Who knows if some twelve-year-old would come out to peek! All fine with her. I also didn't want to offend any women that might be present who didn't know what to expect.

I asked her who the birthday boy was. I can imagine my expression when she told me it was for her son's eighteenth! Oh brother, now what do I do? I asked her if she was sure this was OK, when a pretty young brunette came outside to join her. It was the "boy's" girlfriend. She was friendly, though not as friendly as mom was, but made an attempt to be pleasant nevertheless. I gave both ladies the rundown on what I'd do and what I wouldn't do. Wanted to keep it conservative.....Well, as conservative as a strip tease can be. They agreed.

I went into the backyard and pretended to be from a radio station, telling the young man that he'd won tickets to a concert. I looked in my purse, but couldn't find them. Took off my jacket because I couldn't find them in the pocket either. I asked the guy to help me unzip my skirt; maybe I had them in my garter belt. He looked shocked, but happy. I told him that if he hadn't guessed, I wasn't really from the radio station and that this was his birthday present from mom. The kid loved every minute of it, and by the expressions on his girlfriend, I think he liked it a little too much.

I only danced about twenty minutes and couldn't wait to get out of there. They offered us food and drink but I was way too uncomfortable. It's tough with a family party going on. In my opinion it was not the place for a stripper. Maybe if they'd waited till evening, when the kids and relatives left I would have stuffed my face on all that food!

Note: At every party, I'd go straight for the food. It got so that as we entered someplace, Diana or my bodyguard would just point and tell me where it was!

You've GOT To Be Kidding: I received a call from a good friend. Someone he knew was turning forty and they were having trouble finding a dancer. They specifically wanted a belly dancer. I told him I wasn't a belly dancer but he wanted his friend to call me anyway. I was assured that they would pay well.

When the man called, anyone could easily detect an accent that assured me he was from the Middle East. Now I understood the belly dancing a little better. I made sure he knew that I wasn't one. I was an exotic dancer and could do a sexy little dance for the birthday boy. That was fine with him. He mentioned something about the guys' wife being the one who thought this up, along with him. Hmmmm. ..I wonder if he told her exactly what was going on. I may not know how to belly dance, but I do know that they keep their clothes on! I asked to speak with the wife first.

She called that afternoon and her accent was thicker than his was. Great….hope she'll understand. I explained, telling her that no clothing needed to come off, especially if there was going to be a mixed crowd of men and women. Good with her. She said she'd even bring something for me to try on if I'd like. I was a little confused but oh well.

It was summer and extremely hot. Here's what I wore. From the bottom up: Black thigh highs, lace garter belt with matching black bra and panties. A short, tight mini skirt with a see through mesh top. Over that, a longer skirt, almost to the knee, a buttoned blazer, and only the mesh at the neckline showed. I was warm, but when I got there I realized that I still didn't have enough clothes on.

They were from India and everyone was dressed in their best TRADITIONAL clothing. Not ONE woman even had her legs showing. To make it worse, the place was full of kids! They were clad in traditional garments also. You've got to be kidding? How the heck am I gonna pull this one off? I was a spectacle even before I began to entertain. There were only a few Caucasian people in the room, who were dressed very conservatively. The ladies had longer dresses on and no one had any tight shirts or anything remotely clingy. Not to mention that there were no blondes in the place either, so I stood out like a "marshmallow in a cup of hot chocolate" as a friend of mine put it.

The man who hired me assured me that all would be OK. I told him I'd be very conservative but he had to get every kid out of there and shut the doors. Of course, he would. Then the two wives approached. The wife of the man who hired me and the wife of the birthday boy. They were very friendly and kind which put me at ease, a little. We went into the ladies room and I showed them what I had on. They thought the miniskirt would be okay, after some deliberation but not the mesh shirt. I was to keep the jacket on. *Great, why don't they just throw me in a steam bath with all this black clothing on!* They showed me some beautiful, brightly colored skirts and scarves but I had no idea how to wear them so I stayed with my own clothes.

Went up to the DJ next, who was a family member and gave him some music. He announced that I was "so and so" from a local restaurant, here to present the birthday boy and his wife with a gift certificate for dinner. When they asked him to sit in the middle of the room he must have caught on. He said no! No smile, no expression, just plain, no. His wife put a chair next to him and sat with him. She was so cool! They made him sit and the music went on. I started to dance sexy, in all those layers, and unbuttoned the jacket. I motioned to the wife that I was going to take off the skirt. OK with her. I unzipped the back and gave everyone a peek to see I had something on underneath. Didn't want to give anyone a heart attack! He wouldn't even look, but she sure had fun.

Stripped to the mini and flashed a garter here and there. I was dying of heat by now when four other guys had joined who were tipping so I didn't want to quit just yet. I grabbed one of the long bright scarves and put in around my neck, draping it over my breasts, then took the jacket off. All they could see were bra straps from the back. Much better. The guys wanted more, but I told them I couldn't, given the circumstances. It only lasted fifteen minutes when a few of the ladies were getting offended. I think they were afraid it would go further. Heaven forbid I should show a thigh, so I stopped, thanked everyone and tried to bolt.

The funniest thing was on the way out when a little old lady came up to me with a great big smile, took a few dollars out of the back of my skirt and handed them to me. She said something like, "Don't lose this!" She smiled and patted my rear end! She must have been a trip. To bad she hardly spoke English. She was probably wishing secretly that she were allowed to be that free and bold.

IT GETS BETTER: Some months later, I received a call from, well, someone from the party, wanting to know if I'd entertain a "couple." Why not? I've done that before I told him. He asked "how much." I asked him how long he wanted me to dance when he let me know he wanted more than a dance. Huh? He wanted me to have sex with him in front of his wife. I'd say that's a little further, wouldn't you? Turns out, they wanted a threesome. Don't let those long, conservative outfits fool you! I was the one dressed sexy, and if I was involved with a man, I'd never in a million years want to watch him have sex with someone else, let alone join in!

When I said I wouldn't have sex with the husband, he asked about oral sex. Said he's never experienced it before but his wife would watch. Let's see....uh....no. Anyway, he never called back. Hope he found what he was looking for.

"But You Said Only Twenty Minutes!": My agent, what a bullshitter! Had to work a bachelor party at another fire station. This was over an hour away, in the next state. I didn't have anyone to go with me, as the bodyguard was working, so my friend Diana agreed to go along. We'd have a girl's night together. This will be fun. We got to the first party with no problems. She put the music on for me and let me "do my thing". It was an average party, about twenty-five guys, average tips, average everything. They were nice, but I think it was too early and they weren't drunk enough to let their hair down. Nine o'clock is the best time…Before everyone is smashed, but after they've had a few.

The crowd was happy and I let them know that I couldn't stick around to socialize, which is fun to do especially when there's good food. I had another party to do.

We got in the car and I told Diana where the next one was. She said that it was about an hour and a half away. No way! The agent told me it was twenty minutes away. They were both wrong. It was more like two hours away. We hit the road and after a while ended up on a two-lane highway going, I don't know where. We were too far into it to turn back. Figured we'd just make the best of it and keep going. What a mistake! Diana was even nice enough not to say, "I told you so."

Now realize that I have terrible eyesight, even with correction and my depth perception isn't great. Well, it's dreadful at night, as you'll see. So, here we are, driving along, when we both spot something in the road, in our path. It's a dead animal. I keep driving, figuring we'll just drive over it and it will slide under the car. It was already dead. That would have worked just fine if it was a squirrel, but it was a deer. Not just any deer, a HUGE DEER! Poor Diana kept telling me to get in the other lane, but there was another car nearby and I didn't think there was time. Besides, we can drive over it. Dah….what was her problem anyway.

Next thing I remember is coming up on the deer and realizing too late that it was certainly larger than I'd thought it was. I ended up driving up and over it, into the air and down again, slamming down on the road and screeching to a halt in the emergency lane. Another time I thought she was gonna stop talking to me….after she got through yelling at me. There were terrible rattling noises coming from the trunk and she got very nervous. Fortunately it was just empty bottles that I hadn't returned yet. We were fine, the car was fine and the two of us actually continued on. We are nuts, aren't we?

By the time we got to our destination it was after midnight. Most of the guys had left but the group that was there appeared happy to see us. The contact guy was irritated because the agent said we'd be there at ten. I told him that I had a show at eight thirty, two hours away, so how could I get there by ten? He said he'd take it up with the agent and realized it wasn't my fault.

We walked in and the few guys left were smashed beyond belief. A guy on the floor with a video camera, trying to put it up our skirts greeted us. It was unanimously decided that this wasn't a good idea. He gave us some money for our trouble and we left. Wished I'd listened to Diana in the first place. Now we had nearly a three-hour trek home.

Everything has a meaning, I believe. We learn from all we do. What did I learn from this experience? I still haven't figured that out yet! No one would let me drive anymore after that. Gee….I wonder why?

Another Youngin': I received a request from an acquaintance to dance for a graduation. My friend knew the dad and his son was graduating from college. He thought it would be fun to surprise him and his friends with a dancer.

Another family party. Had to walk in right through the front door, past all the relatives and all the young friends, male and female. I was dressed already so I didn't need to change. Had on a sundress with the sexy lingerie underneath.

Greeted by the "dad" who seemed pleased by what he saw so far, I was ushered downstairs to a recreation room where there was a room full of young men, up to fifteen of them. The few females that were there were sitting and at first it didn't look like they were going to move. Dad pointed out his son and I went over to him, told him I was a surprise from his dad and started the music.

After a couple of minutes and as soon as clothing started coming off, the females left. It was then that I noticed a yearbook and a couple of other things on the table. I asked him where he'd just graduated from and he mentioned his local high school! I was seriously freaked out, but in a room full of people, what do you do? I asked him how old he was and tried not to seem as uncomfortable as I really was. Fortunately he said eighteen. The rest of the guys in the room were between eighteen and twenty, with one being twenty-two.

They all enjoyed themselves and didn't seem to mind a much "older woman" dancing for them. Matter of fact, they seemed to like it. I later found out that the "kid" who graduated kept my photo in his wallet for a year! I learned to ask more questions after this experience.

Quick Money: On a hot, humid, August evening, I had more than one party in the same night. The first party was at a home with a smaller, well-mannered crowd, probably because it was still early. The group was composed mainly of professional men, mostly lawyers and business owners. They were not only well spoken and polite, but they were ample tippers!

After the show, I had some time to spare and asked if I could freshen up. The host gave me a towel and told me to help myself to the shower. Great idea. I had the bodyguard posted outside the door for privacy as well as protection. He poked his head into the bathroom and said that the guys were begging to watch me in the shower. His idea? Charge them ten bucks and let them come in by twos. I ended up taking a very long shower with lots of suds and making extra cash. I left very refreshed!

A Different Twist: Some things you just can't plan for and certainly don't expect. I showed up at a decent size party with two guys. One was working as my bodyguard and one was along for the ride. Both of these guys were friends of mine, especially the one who was along for the ride. We were discussing the music, lighting, etc., with two of the men when out of the blue one asked me a question. "Which one of these guys is the bodyguard?" I pointed to one and said, "He is." The guys comment floored us. "Good, because this other guy is kind of cute!" I've never seen someone so mortified in my life. My poor friend's face turned white! He just looked at the guy and said, "That's not right!"

We couldn't help but tease him the rest of the evening. He stayed far away from the guy who thought he was cute and just kept mumbling and repeating, "That's just not right!" Well, he really was (and still is) cute, but buddy, leave him for us girls!

Same Two Guys: Another bachelor party with the same two guys. All was going well, I'd made my rounds, danced for everyone and the evening was winding down. I was approached by three men from the party and asked if I'd have sex in front of them with the other guy. (The cute one from before) All the bodyguard could do was crack up laughing while our poor friend just looked puzzled as people were looking at him. He walked over to us and asked what was going on. Trying to hold a straight face I told him that they simply wanted us to have sex in front of them. What was his response? "That's just not right!" I'm surprised he still talks to me.

Parties I've Heard About

Oh yeah…"those" parties. They do happen and happen often. The wild, anything goes parties that most women don't want their guys attending. I can't honestly say I've witnessed them but I've talked to plenty of guys I know personally as well as some of the girls who have done them. Here are some things that happen:

*One girl told me she was going to be a "human sundae" at a party. She'd be on a table and would have her body covered with ice cream, chocolate sauce, whipped cream and cherries. The guys would get to come up and lick it off. I'm sure those guys had a blast and she must have made some good money.

*One girl would give the guys a "dildo" show. The dildo's would start small and progressively get bigger with more money being paid each time. She'd occasionally let one of the sober guys use the dildo on her. I think she just liked playing with dildos and figured she'd get paid for it.

*A girl would let the guys get different veggies and things from the fridge and "play" with them for the guys. A carrot, hot dog, zucchini, cucumber and things like that.

*Some girls will let the guy lie on his back with the dollars in their mouth. They'll actually sit on them to get the money. Not very sanitary if you ask me.

*One dancer would get on all fours, have one guy pour champagne down her back and the one at the "other end" would catch it in his mouth. Hmmmm.

*A girl would suck in smoke (not through her mouth), then exhale it in the guys mouth....for a nice fee, I might add. How the hell did she do that?

*Girls have been known to play "find the cherry." They insert it and leave the stem out. The guy has to get it out with his mouth only...no hands. I've heard of this as bedroom foreplay, but at a bachelor party?

*On rare occasions, golden showers are requested. I'm sure the girls charge a lot for that specialty. From what I've heard, the guest of honor is taken into the tub. It's not something that's done on the kitchen floor!
*(Good story to follow)

*Two girls using a double dildo would just go nuts with each other.

*Two girls without a dildo would go nuts with each other.

*Two girls, also without a dildo, would go nuts on the bachelor, best man, and/or whoever paid.

*Some girls will sit in the bathroom while the guys "line up" for hand or blow jobs. Couldn't tell you the charges, but its not that high.

*Some will have sex with the bachelor and/or his friends.

My question: If the guy is getting married, what the hell is he doing having any kind of sex with ANYONE?

"On Golden Pond": An acquaintance I worked with a few times told me about a small party she worked for about five guys who she knew. It was a birthday, I believe. She did the usual strip tease and the men were totally enjoying it when someone brought up the "potty thing," as they put it. They had a discussion while she danced about who liked golden showers. One did while the others said they'd just like to watch a girl pee. No one had ever seen it, close up and in person, only on the internet and pictures. This went on for a while when one spoke up and asked to see it. Since she knew them all and trusted them, she said okay. She ended up peeing in a cup several times for them. The guys were quite happy and paid her well.

Men never fail to amaze me. I know I'd certainly not enjoy watching a guy pee, close up and I have no idea why they like watching a girl. It cracks me up! They apparently talk about it all the time and she was able to fulfill some fantasies that may sound strange to some, but in my opinion are completely harmless. Guys: Keep the beer going and I'm sure she'll keep filling those cups!

Some fun, yet safe things to do:

*Give away a pair of panties or a T-shirt.
*Use body paint and make a print for the guys to keep.
*Rub baby oil on and let the guys watch.
*Shower or wash the baby oil off.

In defense of some of the grooms to be, I hear that many grooms aren't taking part in those activities. Most often it's the guys at the party doing the lining up. Not all best friends are out to get the groom in trouble before his wedding.

A word to all brides to be: If you ever find out your guy participates in something like this, PLEASE, get mad at HIM. The girls who agree to do this have no idea that some of these guys have girlfriends and may not care. It's about money for them. I would think that your guy should have enough restraint to say "no" and if he doesn't, DUMP HIM and find someone who will be faithful.

On the other side of the coin, for some of the true guys out there, I've been to bachelor parties where the groom to be has actually said that he doesn't fool around. I'd assure him that I didn't do that type of a party and not to worry.

A few crazy things I was asked to do, but didn't.

*Once at a party where there was actually a stage, a guy who was more than half drunk approached me with an empty beer bottle. With a smart-ass grin, he handed it to me, BUT he turned it around and gave me the bottom, large side. I knew by the look on his face what he wanted. What to do? Get mad? Throw it at him? Well, there was a roomful and they were tipping well, so I got smart back. I picked up the bottle, looked at him, moving up a couple of feet and said, "Oh, I'll bet I know what you want me to do with this." I pointed to the big end of the bottle. "Yeah," he answered. "Tell you what," I replied as I handed it back to him, bottom end…."You first!" He wiped that smart grin off of his face and all his buddies roared.

*Many times, the guys would ask the bodyguard if I did "extras" for more money. He'd say "no" and more often than not, they didn't press the issue.

*I've been asked to take nude pictures. That one I can understand. There's great extra money in that but I'm just not comfortable at all with the camera.

*Ask if they could videotape. Ooooo……that reminds me.

At an average sized party, a handful of guys asked for some more time. This was a two-girl show where we danced on separate sides of the room, switching off and on. They were specifically interested in seeing us dance "together" and would pay extra money for our time. We agreed on three songs.

We started the music and began our routine. About halfway in, I noticed a guy zooming in with a video recorder. I jumped up and told him that he couldn't do that. The jerk ran out the door with the tape! Thankfully, my bodyguard ran after him. I looked at the few that were still there and just shook my head. "I wouldn't want to be that guy" I thought. It didn't take more than three minutes when the bodyguard was back with tape in hand. The guy was out. Good going. No violence, in case you're wondering. It wasn't necessary with my guard. He was intimidating enough with words alone.

I could go on and on with this section, but this is to entertain you so I won't make it the book that never ends! Let's get into the next section of the "adult industry" which is the phone sex.

Part Two

Talk Dirty To Me

Live, unedited, uninterrupted, one on one sex talk. The phone....a wonderful device where people can say whatever they want or be whoever they want and still remain anonymous. Here are some of the things one can do over the telephone:

*Live out a fantasy.
*Role-play.
*Tell a secret that no one else knows.
*Tell a sexy secret that you don't want anyone else to know.
*Be dominated, and take your punishment!
*Dominate, and punish someone else!
*Talk really nasty, all those naughty words you're not supposed to use in mixed company.
*Have a threesome, indulge.
*Have an orgy, really indulge!
*Be cross-dressed, learn to walk in high heels and of course,
*Good old fashioned naughty sex talk.

Let me start by answering some of the most popular questions I get asked all the time.

Q. Do women ever call?

A. Nope.. Seems like women won't pay for sex talk, even those ladies who prefer other women. About the only women who've called are calling from other phone sex services, checking out the competition and pretending to be interested. As soon as I tell them I need their credit card, they usually make some excuse, say they'll call back or hang up.

Q. Are these men really "playing with themselves?"

A. Yes. That's the idea. It's OK with me. I can't see a thing.

Q. Are they all "weirdoes?"

A. Not usually. Most of the people who ask this are male. No, they're on the average, regular guys from everywhere who just want to have some very safe sex, or, they want to talk about something they're afraid to tell anyone else or can't talk about with their wife or girlfriend.

Q. Do you ever get weirdoes?

A. Yes. Occasionally. I'm not talking about someone with a mental handicap. I mean real weirdoes. There have been a few. Check out the little section entitled simply, "Weirdoes."

Q. How long is an average sex call?

A. A regular sex call is, on average, ten to twelve minutes. I think the guys are pretty turned on by the time they call.

Q. Why would a guy call when all they have to do is look at a movie or book?

A. This question is asked by men who either have never used a phone sex service, never thought about using one, are just curious, and in some cases, really would never use one. Sometimes, people need a "real" person to talk to. Someone who will use their name and talk directly to them, saying exactly what they want to hear. It's more personal.

Q. Do the clients call back?

A. Yes. A lot. I'd say my "call back" rate is about 90 percent. Some call back once a week, some once a month, some call more than once a week.

Q. Do they lie about their looks?

A. I really do get asked this a lot, by men mostly. I really don't know for sure, but I seriously doubt that there are as many eight, nine and ten inch penises out there as they'd have me believe. On the average though, most men I believe are pretty honest. So they may lie 20 pounds or so. Like women don't?

Most Frequently Asked Questions By Clients:

Q. Is that really you in the picture/web?

A. A most understandable question. Even though I'd always print "actual photo" on a print ad, they'd still ask. Not much in the phone sex business is for real so I can't blame them. It could be an "actual photo" of someone else! I've seen different companies with the same girl, same picture, only with a different name. The photos are for sale. I wanted a real and personal business, so I always used my real pictures.

Q. What are you wearing?

A. Another good question. I want things to be believable, so I don't say I'm wearing a red lace teddy at two o'clock in the afternoon. I tell the truth, cause sometimes, little cut off jean shorts and a T-shirt tied in a knot can be more sexy than lingerie. If I'm just out of the shower and in only a towel, or in the middle of undressing, I'll say so. At times, I'm on my hands and knees, cleaning. They really like the "hands and knees" part.

Q. Are you playing with yourself?

A. Oh come on guys. Do you really think that's all I do all day? Some men actually think that the phone sex operators are just nypho's who want to get off all day. A definite myth. If there was no money in it, very few would be doing it. That's a fact.

Q. Do you ever masturbate?

A. All guys want to ask women that one,

Q. When was the last time you had sex?

A. I don't understand why guys want to know this. Guess it goes along with the porn thing. They like to visualize the woman they're talking to with someone and/or themselves.

Q. How does this appear on my credit card?

A. Just threw that in there to see if you're paying attention.

THE PHONE CALLS

I'm going to let you in on all kinds of telephone conversations that I've had with clients. Some are funny, some will have you in stitches on the floor, some are very naughty, some are naughty and graphic, some are weird, others are even more weird, and some you'll have to read more than once because you won't believe it. The stories are in no particular order, so just enjoy. Also, names and descriptions were changed for privacy, to protect the innocent and in a lot of cases, to protect the guilty!

The average call is pretty generic. Most times, the client is watching a porn or flipping through a naughty magazine. They may be looking at my website or run across a photo I've sent them. Sometimes they just wake up "in a mood." Then they call me. Over fifty percent of the phone sessions are what I call "normal" or "average," meaning they're about a man, a woman and sex between them both. Ages vary tremendously with the youngest caller being eighteen and the oldest I've encountered, in his seventies.

During some of these calls, the guys will actually say things like, "Oh, you smell so good," "I can taste you," "I can feel you," etc. It's amazing what some can "feel" over the phone. All I can say is I'm glad that they can enjoy themselves so much to actually feel something. I'm not speaking for all women, but it's harder to fantasize about things like that and actually "feel" it. I think in general, men are more into audio and visual than women are. Women appreciate a real touch, the real smell of a man's cologne or a kiss. Not just a fantasy.

You'll notice that in many calls I'll refer to myself as the object of their desires. That's not always the case. There are those who call specifically to speak to me, they have photos or have been on the Internet. There are also those who could care less what I look like and have their own ideas. I'm just role-playing.

If you're a guy reading this book, you'll surely discover some of your own fantasies and fetishes here. Hopefully, some of you will realize that your thoughts are not all that different. Many men think the same as you do.

If you're a woman reading this, believe it. This is really what a lot of guys are thinking about. Some will share it with you, but most won't, either for fear of rejection or that you'll laugh and think they're nuts. Remember that most of it is just fantasy. That's why it's done on the phone. When asked if some of the "different" fantasies would really be acted out, eighty percent say "no" or "I doubt it." Sometimes, fantasies are best left at just that.

You'll read about all sorts of phone conversations and fantasies in this section. From the naughty to the nasty, the nice guys to the wild. What they say, what they want, how they say it and all their secrets ….. Exposed. I hope you have as much fun reading as I have putting this section together.

The "Normal" Calls:

These are the standard calls. The regular, dirty phone sex calls that you'd expect to hear about. The hot and heavy breathing and the naughty sex talk. I really shouldn't use the word "dirty." It's not. It's just sex talk, only very explicit. In relating some of the stories, I will use the real words that they use, like the "f" word, to get the point across and at other times I'll use my own translations.

Take my nine inches: This guy called me about every two weeks, asking if I'd like to "play." Whether I'd be in the middle of cooking dinner, writing this book, or weeding the garden, my answer would always be,

"Of course!" His conversation would start by all the naughty things he'd like to do. He'd speak in an accent, as he was of Asian decent and as he became more turned on, his accent would get thicker, sometimes making it difficult for me to understand. However the word "fuck" with any accent is understandable. He'd get into lots of foreplay and would say, "Now suck my dick." "Ok now, take his nine inches." *I'm five feet tall....what the hell do I want with nine inches!. Another guy in the "nine inch and over" club.*

The funniest thing was at the end, when he was finished he'd say: "OK…it is done." I think it was his foreign background and language difference, but it sure sounded amusing to hear. Actually, he seemed to be a pretty nice guy, just someone who got a little lonely at times and found someone he liked to look at and related to.

The Always Sexy, Bubble Bath: Some callers aren't specific. They just say they want to be turned on. If they are of a sensual nature, which I find out subtly by asking a few questions, one of the fantasies I like is the bubble bath. There are so many variations of this one, but here's one I like.

A hot steamy bubble bath is drawn, complete with candles, fluffy towels and champagne. Berries and grapes are in a bowl nearby to heighten the pleasure. He gets into the tub. When he's comfortable, I take off my little satin nightie and stand there in nothing but a pair of heeled slippers. I give him his glass of champagne, slide off my slippers and join him in the tub. We take sips and I feed him the berries. He returns the treatment. Then I take a handful of bubbles and begin to rub his neck and chest while I kiss him. I get on my knees, press my breasts against his cheeks and reach over to get some bubbles on his back. I tell him to look in the mirror at my rear end, which is covered in bubbles, as I kneel up. Now, watch as the bubbles melt away, exposing a nice, round, tanned bottom. He caresses that rear with his sudsy hands and licks those breasts softly.

He feels a hand running down his chest and into the water, feeling how hard he is becoming. Mmmmm….how nice. We're both getting very turned on now so we stand up and wrap up in the fluffy towels. The rest will take place in the bedroom. He carries me to the bed and the towels are unwrapped. With hair still dripping wet, we get into some nice, sensual oral sex. He wants to drive me wild and I want to do the same, so we take turns pleasing each other until we bring it all together and make love for a wonderful long time. *This is for the sweet type guy whose in a romantic, make love kind of mood. Not intended for those who want a wild headboard banging night!*

Come For Me: I guess many guys are into audio as much as video. "I want to hear you come," is a popular request. So…..I ask them what they'd do if they were here to make that possible. The usual answer is oral sex. OK…I ask them to describe exactly how they'd do it. Gotta tell ya, I get some pretty good responses. Seems that the guys who are into giving oral sex like to take their time and get just as much enjoyment out of pleasing the woman as they do getting pleasure. Knowing they're making a woman hot gets them even hotter.

When the call is nearing an end and they want to hear the girl come on the phone, most guys can't contain themselves. A little note for the guys reading this, Women really CAN fake it….. VERY WELL.

The Police Officer Fantasy: A guy in his twenties called and was a little hesitant about what he'd like. I could tell he had something specific on his mind so I coaxed him to tell me what it was. He said he'd always had a fantasy about a lady police officer and how the uniform turned him on. He wanted me to role-play a very naughty cop who would take advantage of him. I came up with this:

I'm the lady officer who pulls over a gentleman for speeding. I tell him that if he gets one more ticket, he'll lose his license. He pleads his case that he needs to get to work and promises not to speed again. I toy with him a while about giving him the ticket when he offers me money. A bribe? What kind of cop would I be if I took a bribe? I tell him he can do better than that, as I lean into his window, exposing definite cleavage. I drop my pen in his lap and pick it up, brushing his crotch. Now he gets the message and asks to take me for a drink. No…That would never do. I'm on duty.

He's afraid of me so I take off my hat. Long blond hair falls over my shoulders and down my back. He still seems nervous so I hop into the car with him and take off my uniform. I tell him that seeing me in nothing but my satin underwear should assure him I'm just a woman and won't do anything to harm him. He finally relaxes and asks to see my breasts. I take the bra off and tell him to show me what he's got. Before long, we're both naked. I give him oral sex and then we fog up the windows having sex in his car. By the way, he gets a break and doesn't get a ticket. *Maybe he really owned the nine inches!*

Naughty Nurse: Yes. All those things you hear about the naughty nurse are true in fantasies. Guys love it. The sexy looking nurse coming into the room and giving the patient more than a sponge bath.

On one call, I told a "patient" that I was shutting the door to give him a once over check. He was only in his bottoms. I checked his temp, blood pressure, and pulse, making sure to rest his arm very close to my large DD breasts. *Oh, now this really IS a fantasy!* He tells me that his back and shoulders are sore, so I start to rub them, leaning over and whispering, "How does that feel?" *How would you feel with double D's pressed up against your back? It could make his problems worse!*

He tells me I smell nice and am the prettiest nurse there. I say he's a very handsome patient and it goes from there. He reaches for my uniform and I let him unbutton it, all the way down. He requests that the hat stays on and the hair stays up. I undress down to my white garters and stockings and little panties. We kiss for a while when he pulls me on top of him for some great sex. We have to be quiet so I won't get fired. From the looks of things, I'd say this patient doesn't need to be in the hospital anymore!

For all you real nurses out there: Don't worry, we know that no one really wears heels, garters and stockings on the job. That's as silly as those

1950 commercials where the housewife had on heels, dresses and pearls to clean her floor!

The Best Friend: This one is an ego boost for the guys who enjoy this type of fantasy/role play. The situation is this: I'm bringing back some CD's to my boyfriend's house but he's not home from work yet. His best friend and roommate are, so we start chatting as usual. He notices that I'm disturbed about something and I confide in him that I'm just not happy with my boyfriend. Things on a personal level aren't good. We don't have sex anymore and I get no attention. It's making me feel unattractive.

The best friend tells me how beautiful I am and that any guy would be thrilled to have sex with me, including him. "Really?" I say shyly. He moves closer and strokes my hair for "comfort." I tell him his touch feels so good and that I wish my boyfriend would touch me like that. His hands move from my hair to my neck and down my back. When he sees me respond he moves to the sweater, the buttons, the jeans and the bra. You know the rest.

After we have tremendous sex, I tell him how wonderful it was and how many orgasms I had, which I've never had before. I feel so guilty but I must see him again, very soon. *Like I said this purely an ego boost. This fantasy is ALWAYS their request.*

I Want You, NOW! Some guys I speak to would like their women to be more aggressive. On the average, the guys who want an aggressive female in fantasy usually don't have it in real life.

How about this: He's already in bed, reading a book when I come in from a "sexy nightie" party at my girlfriend's house. I slip into the bathroom and put on a very seductive red satin number with the heels to match. I walk upstairs with two chilled glasses of wine and a tiny bottle of lotion tucked in the side of my G-string.

When I enter the room, he looks, smiles, puts his book down, and asks if I had a good time. I say I did and now I'm going to have a better time and so is he. I take the book off the bed, sit right on top of him and give him some wine, almost ordering him to drink up. While he's sipping, I pull the covers down, take the little bottle of lotion, start rubbing it on his nipples, and then lick it off. *By the way, it's lickable lotion.* Then the covers come off and the lotion is rubbed all over his very hard penis. Mmmmm....how tasty. I put the lotion on my breasts and let him taste. I tell him I want him now and just sit right down on his hard penis. I get on top, take the control and the sex is on the wild side. He loves it.

Be A Slut: This is actually more popular than I would have thought. I don't think any guy would really want this, but a role-play would be fun.

One guy in particular just loves this and is rather detailed about what he wants. He'll tell me what to say and the sluttier it is; the more turned on he gets. He tells me to say how "I love cock, I love to fuck, I'll take any cock, I'm a slut, I'm a dirty whore, I'm a nasty dirty slut, etc." He'll then go a little further and ask me if I'd ever had my uncle or my brother. I don't go into incest fantasies, so I turned it around and said: "I'll do your brother and your uncle." That worked. I told him that he could watch me take them both on at the same time.

After the brother and Uncle I'd go out on the street and pick up three more guys and do them too. He loved that one. All through my talking he'll keep asking me to tell him what a slut I am. After the allotted time, he'll politely say he's going to go now because he's going to explode.

I don't understand why anyone would fantasize about someone like that, but as long as he knows it's just a fantasy and not really how I am, that's okay. Gotta watch that stuff. Someone might think I really act like that....someone with a "Jack the Ripper" fantasy!

Be My Neighbor:

On more than a few occasions I've been asked to be the seductive neighbor next door. Here are a couple of the fantasies:

Car Trouble: I'm outside, struggling with my car, wearing little short shorts and a bikini top as it's such a hot day outside. My next door neighbor is watching me from his window and enjoying the view every time I bend over and show a little cheek. He starts to get turned on and decides to make a move. He comes outside and asks me if I'd like some help. Naturally, he fixes the car and I'm very thankful. I invite my nice neighbor in for a cold drink and proceed to tell him how much I want to thank him for his help.

I take my bikini top off and climb on his lap. He's surprised by my aggressive behavior and, tells me that he's wanted this for a long time also. We then proceed to undress and have wild sex all over the house. OK boys, 'fess up. You've thought about that one, haven't you?

Your Wife's Not Home?: I knock on my neighbor's door to return something I borrowed form his wife. Since her car isn't in the driveway, I have some idea that she may not be home. Oh that's right, I'd forgotten that she'd be on a business trip for two days. When the husband politely invites me in, I change from the nice neighbor to the seductress, sitting on the sofa in a tight skirt. I've just come from the office so I'm still in business attire. I take off my jacket and loosen two buttons on my blouse, revealing a little lace on my bra. I make sure he sees my thigh high stockings and flash him a little black lace panty.

*Note: Guys, remember this IS a fantasy. You try wearing thigh high stockings in an office with the rubber that keeps them up pressed against your leg all day. Combine that with heels and you'll have one uncomfortable lady!

Back to the story: When I know he's looking and obviously interested, I confess that I've always though he was so sexy and we take it from there. He comments on how he wishes his wife would wear those sexy stockings, heels and lace panties. Being the good neighbor that I am, I decide to show him the panty, along with the bra, and eventually what's underneath it all. We have passionate sex over and over in his bed.

This is such a common fantasy, but another one of those that will more than likely remain just that, a fantasy. Think of the consequences of this being a reality? I mean, the wife could come home unexpectedly, a nosy neighbor could tell, the delivery guy could walk in, etc. The possibilities are endless!

More Tanning Lotion Please?: I'm the sexy girl next door, sunning outside in a tiny thong bikini, rubbing oil all over myself while the man next door is watching. I make it a point to rub the oil on the inside of my thighs and over my nearly exposed breasts. When I catch his eye, I smile and motion for him to come over. He of course, says yes. I hand him the oil and ask him to rub it on my back, my legs, and eventually over my tanned rear end.

When I notice him becoming excited, I turn around, reach for him and slide him out of his clothing, right there in my back yard, in broad daylight. We try to hide under our towels on the lawn chair but we're so turned on that we don't care who's watching. We have oral sex in a sixty-nine position while the sun beams down on our bare bottoms. We make so much noise outside that the neighbors begin to watch. Nothing matters and we continue having sex right there on the chair.

*Another Note: Most guys with the sexy neighbor fantasy don't really have a sexy neighbor at all. I've asked them!

The Older Woman:

This topic appears to be a favorite. A lot of these calls are website generated, most likely because I am quite honest about my age and always have been. They'd read the age on the site and like the idea.

So I'm over forty, well over 40, not too far from fifty. I'm fortunate enough to carry it with some ease; I'd like to think. In turn, a lot of younger guys like this type of fantasy. I mean young too! Nineteen, twenty, and up to twenty-five being very common. Why? Lots of reasons. They say that older women know what they want and are secure. Some are…some not.

In most cases, these very young guys would not be likely to ask a much older woman out on a date or become involved in real life. In my opinion only and personally speaking, it wouldn't lead anywhere with someone still in college who hasn't started their life yet, and someone who is old enough to be a grandparent. Nothing against relationships with a serious age difference, it does depend on the situation. A lot of younger guys would like the experience and patience of a mature lady. So, here's how some of these fantasies went.

Be My Roommate's Mom: I'm the mom, paying a visit to my college son, but I arrive an hour early. Thinking he might be there anyway, I go up to his dorm room where his roommate greets me. I'm told that my son won't be back for a while, but I'm welcome to wait. The roommate shows me some photos he's taken for his photography class, which means that we're sitting next to each other on a love seat.

He tells me I smell nice. I say thank you and he tells me that I look nice also. I again accept the compliment. He moves a little closer. I hear his breathing becoming stronger and feel his breath on my neck making the hair tickle my face. *Yeah, this story moves fast, but after all, we only have fifteen minutes!* I move my hair seductively away, exposing my perfumed neck. At that point, I look over and tell him I think he's very handsome and charming. He asks if he can kiss me. Just once. Since he's SO handsome, I just can't say no and I let him. This leads to more passionate kissing.

Before I know it, he has my blouse unbuttoned and my skirt up. He gets up and locks the door, assuring me that my son is really going to be out two hours. He comes back to the love seat and throws his clothing off and on to the floor. Things get very hot and heavy and we have sex three times before we put ourselves back together. The affair will go on the next time I visit...*Of course, I get much more detailed on the calls.*

The Pool Guy: I hire a young man to take care of my pool this summer. *I wish. I have to do the damn thing myself!* While he works, I like to walk around in a bikini or in this case a little white sundress that is sheer. I make sure the sun is hitting the dress while I bring him an ice tea so that he can see the little lines of my G-string panties. *Do you notice that I'm the one who is always doing the pursuing?* I tell him to take a break, as it's so warm. He sits facing me in a comfortable chair with a mirrored coffee table between us. I question him and ask his age. He says he's twenty. I comment that, "If I were only twenty years younger..." to which he says how much he likes me now. I return the compliment and casually put my foot on top of the table, moving my leg back and forth so that he can get a peek up my dress. *I'm such a slut, aren't I?*

When I catch him watching, I look him in the eye as I take the dress and put it between my legs to cover his view. I ask if he'd like to follow me inside and help bring in the glasses and pitcher. He immediately gets up to help. I notice how hard he is through his shorts.

Inside the kitchen, I begin to wash the glasses when he comes up behind me and pushes his hard body against me (hard, being the word here). I turn around and kiss him. He picks me up on to the counter and we have crazy sex right then and there.

Give Me Instructions: One young man of twenty called to say he loves older women and had a fantasy where he'd masturbate in front of a lady as she gave him instructions. I'm a girl and not sure I could really instruct a guy but I tried. (I do believe he followed my coaching to the letter)

I told him to sit comfortably in a big chair while I sit opposite on another. He's instructed to relax, sit back, watch and listen to me. I hike up my little skirt, run my hands up my leg and tell him to rub himself through his pants. *I have to give him a sexy visual, you know.* I make him do everything for about a minute while I talk to him and say, "That's so good," "Oh yeah, that's it" and "Keep going." I direct him now to unzip his pants and reach in but only touching his underwear. No skin yet. While he does this, I unbutton my sweater a little, lean forward and show him lots of cleavage. *OK, so I don't have LOTS of cleavage. I can fantasize too!* I lean back and tell him it's okay now to touch his penis. "Rub it now, but don't grab it. Just rub it." He's beginning to sigh a little now. Really.

Now I tell him to start stroking it, very slowly, stopping just under the head. He does this for a while and should now rub his fingers up and over the head until it starts to get wet. At this point, I reach over to him, take one of his hands and squeeze some lube into his palm, gently putting his hand back on his penis. He's told to go a little faster now. He's now groaning, so I tell him to stop and rub his b's. He's groaning louder so I make him do it faster. I tell him how throbbing hard he is and that I want him to shoot it all over himself. He should also ask permission to come and when he does, I want to hear it…loud. He does what he's told. He did well in "Masturbation 101," don't you think?

The young photographer: I have an appointment to have some photos taken for my husband's birthday. They are to be on the sexy side. I wear a saloon girl costume with stockings, garters and a low cut dress complete with ruffles at the bottom, a corseted waist and push up bra. My nice sized breasts are just popping out of the top. Perfect.

My young, handsome photographer talks to me as he sets things up. I look around the room and notice all the pictures he's taken and tell him he's done amazing work for someone so young. *Yes, I'm fishing for info here.* He tells me he's not that young, he's all of 24. I tell him that my son is 23 and he's amazed. Says his mom isn't nearly as young looking and is my age. Flattery just might get you somewhere!

Now start more compliments, and the camera. He takes pictures, telling me to pull the sleeves off of my shoulders. A little more, a little bit more, now just another inch. Now most of my breast is showing. He puts his camera down for a moment and comes in to adjust a big pillow I'm leaning on. He moves my hair, "just so," when I realize my breast is exposed. He tells me I have beautiful breasts and should let him photograph them. I'm too shy for that, so he puts the camera back, comes over to sit with me and talk. He softly talks to me and moves the ruffles on my dress up to expose most of my leg. He tells me to lie down against the pillows and moves the dress up around my rear end. He takes a few pictures.

Now he comes back over to me and crawls right on top, pushing my skirt up with his hands. This guy wastes no time! He slides off his clothes and we begin having sex. The best part is that later, he shows me all the pictures that the camera was randomly snapping as we were getting it on.

Note: If you're wondering who came up with this one, it was a combination. He gave me some input and I took over.

The Younger Woman

Believe it or not, I've had three times as many men call to request an older woman rather than younger. Maybe it's because I don't advertise as a "barely legal" phone sex girl. Seems the "grass is always greener" and the young guys want older women as the older guys like younger ones.

Many times, the younger girl fantasy is about the guy being the dad and the girl being a friend of the daughter. Very popular. Most of the guys requesting this are admittedly over forty. I think they enjoy the idea of a younger girl finding them attractive and desirable. Now don't lie guys, many of you think about it. Here are some examples:

Everyone Went To Bed, but I Can't Sleep: Young, college freshman is sleeping over her friend's house. It's midnight and everyone went to bed. The girlfriend who lives there, her younger brother and the mom are all sound asleep. The pretty, young coed walks downstairs to get something to drink. She's wearing a nightshirt that is clingy around her tight rear end, showing the lines of her little bikini panties underneath. She has no bra on and her small breasts are young and firm. The dad is working in his den and can't help but look at her in the dim light that is in the kitchen. He's been looking at her for months but has never seen her wearing so little.

The pretty girl walks by the den, stops to say hello and the dad asks her if she's okay. "Yes Mr. Jones. I just can't sleep." He notices that she looks upset and invites her into the den. She sits down on a comfortable sofa and says she broke up with her boyfriend today. "All he does is go to parties and drink. He's going nowhere and is so immature. I wish he was smart and mature, like you." The dad is flattered and tells her that he was the same way when he was young. "Maybe you need an older man," he suggests. She reveals that she's always dreamed about an older man and wondered what it would be like to have sex with someone as handsome and mature as Mr. Jones.

Mr. Jones is feeling confident now and tells her to come on over. He says how beautiful she is and how he'd love to see her perfect body. She removes her nightshirt and it drives the man wild. He wants her so bad now. The door is closed and they must be quiet, so as not to wake anyone in the house. She promises not to tell her friend and he promises not to let his wife find out. They have a passionate night of sex on the sofa in the den. I think she should stop calling him "Mr. Jones" at this point!

Let Me Seduce You: Another "dad" fantasy. This time, the young girl comes over to visit her friend, but finds only the dad home. The friend is detained somewhere. Matter of fact, she won't be home for a couple of hours. The girl tells the dad she has to finish a paper and needs help. It's for History and she has so much trouble with that class. Since the dad is a teacher, perhaps he'd be kind enough to help her. "Of course I'll take the time to help you." Before the dad can get up and go to the table, the girl sits right next to him on the love seat. She's so happy, how can he refuse her.

As they "study" she gets even closer, says she's warm and unbuttons part of her sweater. Her body language is screaming for sex and the dad knows it. He's a little uncomfortable but turned on at the same time. The girl senses that he is intrigued with her and puts her hand on his leg, asking him why he looks so fidgety. He says he's fine. She closes her book and tells him that she thinks he's helped enough and wants to thank him. Leaning over and giving him a hug, she presses her breasts against him. She tells him he's SO handsome and she's always fantasized about him, since she was sixteen. Now that she's eighteen, it's OK.

He just can't help himself. He takes her upstairs to his own bedroom where they enjoy themselves for a long time. The girl tells him that he's the best because he takes his time and knows how to treat a woman, unlike the boys she's been with. They make plans to meet again the next week. *Meaning he'll call back in a week.*

Note: In talking to men of all ages, it's pretty common knowledge that the "older" men do take their time, like to please the woman, like to touch and caress and prolong everything. They make love more than they have sex. I think a woman of any age appreciates that. Keep up the good work!

I'll Be Your Teacher: Yeah, the student/teacher fantasy. One guy likes to be the college professor with the young, seductive, freshman student. She comes to see him after class because she has a problem she'd like to talk over. She just can't grasp his class and is so worried that she starts to cry, right on his shoulder. He comforts her.

She stops crying but keeps her head on his shoulder, telling him how safe and secure he makes her feel, then whispers in his ear how attractive he is and how turned on she gets when she's near him. He doesn't know what to do at first and tries to brush it off, telling her it's just a schoolgirl crush. She insists that she's no schoolgirl, is a real woman and will prove it.

Before he knows it, his pants are unzipped and she's under his desk. He has become so turned on now that he just can't say no to this young, beautiful student. As she stands up, he pulls up her skirt and caresses her beautiful bottom with his hands. He has her gently sit on him and they have great sex right there in his classroom. *She shut the door beforehand in case you're wondering.*

Teacher Two: Another student/teacher fantasy. This time the teacher isn't as innocent and the student isn't as bold. It's the other way around for this guy. Same situation. The girl comes in after class for some extra help. The teacher gives her the good news that she's improving so much that her grade went way up and she'll pass with flying colors. She is thrilled and says she'll miss coming for extra help because she likes the teacher so much. He responds by telling her he will miss her too. He has cherished looking at her pretty face, gorgeous hair and the cute clothes she wears. He loves the way her shirts show just a little bit of her firm tummy, as he touches her. She is surprised but likes it.

He goes on to play with the strap on her shirt, pulling it down and saying how much he's dreamed of being this close to her. He kisses her and tells her to relax. She begins to enjoy the touch of this handsome professor who's her dad's age. She kisses him back and gets very turned on. They end up having sex on his desk. *Don't know if the door was shut this time.*

Note: The above students are fictitious so please don't call me and ask for numbers!

Voyeurism

People like to watch. That's all there is to it. If anyone doesn't agree, just look at the sales of adult literature, magazines, videos, etc. Good money is paid to see "live sex shows" and those "porn booths" where one can watch a girl by herself. Some like to peek while the person or people don't know they are being watched and others like to be seen and heard. Then there are the ones who want to join in. Here are a few samples:

Peeping Tom (or Tim, or John, etc.): VERY POPULAR. Numerous guys, all along the same theme brought this fantasy to me. The peeping Tom. Kinda makes you wonder!

I'm in my bedroom, just out of the shower wearing only a towel with my hair pinned up. My curtains are very sheer and the neighbor across the street is watching me. First, I drop the towel and stand in front of my mirror, naked. Then, I unpin my hair and shake it all over my shoulders. The man is getting turned on while watching me.

Next, I get lotion and rub it all over my body. First the breasts, then arms, shoulders and legs, bending over to reach them. I lay the towel on the bed and sit down on it to finish lotioning. He can't see as well now, so he gets closer to the window and peeps in for a better look. As he nearly puts his nose to the glass, he sees me lotion my inner thighs. You can figure where it goes from there. I rub the lotion all over a "freshly shaven pussy" and he gets so turned on that he has to masturbate while he's viewing. He's careful not to make any noise and stays outside the window until I dress for bed. He goes back to his house and I never know a thing. *By the way, I have a very nice, respectful neighbor across the street who'd never do such a thing!*

Note: Ladies, next time you're in your room alone, check your shades before you drop that towel!

The Voyeur 2: This guy also wanted to be a peeping Tom, but he wanted to get caught. Of course, I wouldn't mind it at all and even welcome him inside the house for some playtime. *Okay, that's really pushing the fantasy button.* Here's how I handled this one.

The peeper is working on my lawn and over hears me on the phone telling a friend that I won't be ready for an hour and will start dressing now. *He must have been planting flowers, 'cause he surely wouldn't have heard anything over the lawn mower!* He looks in the window without being noticed and waits for me to undress. He watches as I strip down to my bra and panties. Sexy red lace. I look through my closet, pick out a tiny black dress and put it on the bed. Next come some sheer stockings. As I bend over to reach the drawer, I notice a glimpse of him in my mirror.

I walk to the window and say in a very sexy voice, "I know you're there. Why don't you come on in."

He enters the house and I encourage him to come into my bedroom. When he walks in, I'm laying on the bed, totally naked. I tell him to undress and come over to me. He climbs on the bed and I toss all the clothing on the floor telling him that my friend can wait. I'd rather be with him. We have sex in many different positions and are both completely satisfied, for now anyway. This guy loves to talk in detail about the different positions and how each feels. That's another of his turn on's.

Note: I wonder if this ever really happens? If anyone out there knows for sure, write me, will you?

The Football Player & The Cheerleader: This man gave me the title and I came up with the fantasy. He simply said that he wanted to be a voyeur with young cheerleaders and a big, black football player. I put on my thinking cap and came up with the following:

The client/voyeur has attended a college game and doesn't leave the locker room when he's supposed to. Curious as to what really goes on in there, he hides and watches.

In comes a cheerleader. Pretty girl with gorgeous legs and long golden brown hair, pulled back in a ponytail. She's bending down, getting things out of her locker when in comes a huge football player. The client specifically requested a "big cock." He's only wearing a pair of sweat pants and the voyeur can see his huge penis bulging already.

The big black football player comes from behind and grabs the cheerleader around the waist, pushing his hard body into hers. She likes this. The voyeur is watching and getting hot so he starts rubbing himself. *That was his idea.* The football player removes his pants to expose his huge; I mean HUGE cock, which she immediately starts to suck. *That was his idea too.* The big man picks her up, takes her panties off and puts her against a wall where he bangs the heck out of her. They finish when my voyeur does. *Good thing the big football player never notices him or he'd be a splat on the locker room wall.*

I Love To Watch My Wife: Believe it or not, I've heard this fantasy, almost exact from more than a few guys. In reality, I think that most men would freak out, but others get turned on. Since this is "make believe," we'll have to guess how many would indeed enjoy the following as reality. With this theme, I'm generally the one who makes up the story, unless there's something specific they want.

A man comes home from a business trip and sees a co-worker's car in the driveway. When he enters the house, no one is in the kitchen or living room, as he'd expect. He walks upstairs and hears some noises. The bedroom door is open and he sees his wife on the bed wearing lingerie. She's tall and slender with light hair and light skin. *This is what the client told me his wife looked like.* He peeks in a little more and sees his co-worker giving his wife oral sex. Her legs are wrapped around his neck and he's going at it like crazy. He's black, very black, with smooth chocolate skin, an almost shaved head, a rippled chest and a huge cock. *No, this isn't the same guy as in the previous story, but again, the choice of a big black man was the client's.*

She tells him she loves his big cock and wants it. He puts her legs in the air and gives her all of it. She tells him that he's so much bigger than her husband is, loves it, and wants it harder. She savors every minute of it. Then he pulls it out and comes all over her breasts.

The client specifically said he wanted to watch the big black man "shoot" all over his wife which was another big turn on for him. He also was the one who mentioned how small he was in comparison to the other man. He'd get hotter with every mention of the other mans huge penis compared to his small one. He'd also ask detailed questions about what the man was doing with his wife, which really made him flip. Different…..

Note: I've gotta know guys. If anyone out there would really enjoy this let me know

They Can See Us: This one was my idea. A guy called and said he'd always fantasized about being watched somewhere kind of public. Hmmmm….How about a camera? He liked that idea so I came up with this:

We've been at a party in a posh hotel and are heading upstairs to our room in, yes, the elevator. We start to kiss and his hand goes up the slit in my long dress exposing a nice little lace thong panty. Even though we can't see it, we know there's a camera in the elevator and that we're probably being watched. He doesn't care. He pushes the "stop" button and off comes the suit jacket. Down go the pants and up goes the skirt. Mmmm…. a quickie between floors. Detail of the moans and groans are mentioned as well as the loud echo in the elevator.

After composing ourselves, he pushes the elevator button again, making it stop on the wrong floor, as we know the management will most likely be waiting to scold us for our naughty behavior. *Fined for indecent exposure is more like it.*

The phone client was satisfied with this little adventure, said it sounded like fun and wanted to try it sometime. That's up to him but I wouldn't advise doing this for real.

The Voyeur….Reversed: This client wanted to be watched by someone he just met. No problem, but I needed more specifics. Watched, doing what? He said, "playing with himself." Here's what my crazy imagination concocted.

A group of people are staying at a hotel for a wedding. I've had my eye on a tall, handsome man throughout the evening and he's had his eye on me. We danced a few times, had a few drinks and took some instant pics of each other as well as the rest of the group.

It's getting late and I notice that the tall man has disappeared. Friends tell me he went up to his room. I notice that the guy he's sharing the room with is still partying, so I get a bottle of wine and go upstairs. As I approach his room I see the door opened a little. I peek in and see him playing with himself while looking at the picture he took of me. I watch him for a little bit and then decide to quietly walk in. He is surprised but happy to see me. I tell him, "Why don't you let me do that," walk over to him and take over with my hands, then my mouth while he watches in the mirror. He returns the attention. We finally shut and lock the door and are sure that the people in the next room can hear us banging the headboard against the wall for a long time.

Now on the phone, I went into more details along with some very naughty words, but I'm trying to condense it here. Don't know about you, but that headboard banging in hotel drives me nuts, especially when the hotel neighbors wake you at 4:00 AM!

Watch Me Play: This gentleman in his late thirties likes to be watched and laughed at. You're probably wondering how I find out that someone likes to be laughed at, right? They don't always tell me. They give hints. The first time I spoke with him he'd say things like, "Are they watching me? Are they laughing and giggling?" I could tell by the way he asked that it was something he wanted, so I incorporated it in his tale and it worked.

Here's his newest fantasy….OK, so it was my idea. I'm working at a nightclub as an exotic dancer. I finish a private dance with him and excuse myself to go change before dancing for him again. I tell him he's welcome to sit and wait on the comfortable love seat and that I'll be only a few minutes. Before I go, I leave behind my panties.

When I return, I catch sight of him rubbing his penis through his pants while looking at the panties. He picks them up and rubs them over his nose and mouth. He doesn't see me, so I continue to watch. As he gets more and more turned on, he unzips his pants and exposes himself. At that point I can't help but giggle loud enough for him to hear but he ignores it. Knowing I'm watching turns him on even more. He starts stroking himself faster and I call a friend over to watch. She actually laughs out loud and we know for sure he hears us both. He doesn't care. Before long there are four of us observing. He goes even faster now and the more we giggle the harder he strokes. He can't contain himself any longer and comes all over himself. The End.

Sometimes you just have to know what they want. The above client preferred details about what everyone was thinking and saying about him behind his back. That was his turn on, whereas another might like details of what the girls looked like and what they were wearing.

Public Places

Some people have a thing for public places. It's not uncommon for couples to make love in public. The elevator, the beach, the phone booth, the rides at the amusement park, the car, the dressing room and public rest rooms, not to mention the airport and airplanes. So it's also not all that uncommon for some people to want to masturbate in public, although I must say, so far I've only heard that from men.

Here are some stories of phone conversations may or may not have really taken place in a common area.

Let's Get Public: This is a three in one story. Same guy, three different scenarios. Thing is….he really does them. Sex in public places is old hat and not that odd, in fantasy and reality, but this guy twists things a bit.

#1—His office: He called me from his office and wanted to play while at work. Now, I'm picturing a guy in his private office, behind a desk with his pants unzipped, which is how it started out. Then he tells me to "order" him to take his pants off. I told him to take his pants off. He said he needed to take off his shoes and socks first. I heard the shoes drop. Now I told him to play with himself under the desk and asked him if his door to the office was locked. He said it wasn't. I told him to get up and lock it.

Now, I'm imagining a young guy trying to hold his pants up with one hand, the phone on his ear, rushing to lock the door before someone walks in. He didn't want to lock it. Instead he asked me to "tell" him to go out into the hallway. I didn't want to order him to do something so dumb. All I told him was to be careful because if he got caught, he'd not only get fired, but also probably arrested. At this point I heard the door open and it sounded like he was in another part of his office, but I still wasn't sure he was really doing this. He could have been in his home office, just fantasizing, which would have been fine with me.

Next he wanted me to "order" him to sit in the middle of the hallway and play with his penis. He'd say how great it would be if the ladies in the office could see him. Now I'm wondering how nuts he really is. I told him he was ordered to stand up only, in case someone did come by. He said he was walking toward the end of the hall. Now I was getting nervous! All the while, he was describing how hard his "throbbing penis" was and how excited he was to be in public. Well, if I hadn't believed him up until this point, my mind was changed abruptly when he said that someone was coming and I actually heard ladies voices talking. I told him to get the hell back in his office right away. No. He wanted to "jerk off" in the hallway. OK….it's your job, not mine. Have a ball. He supposedly did just as he said, then ran back in his office as fast as possible saying he had to go get dressed before anyone came in. Good time to think of that!

#2—His car: He called me while in his car, driving. I don't know where he was going, if anywhere. I think he just enjoys public situations. I told him it was okay to play in the car but that he was to pull in somewhere after a few minutes.

This guy has a few key words that particularly turn him on. He likes to talk about his "big, throbbing penis head" and asks if I'd like to see it. Oh yes. Absolutely. He tells me he's taking it out of his dress pants and looking at how hard it's getting. I told him not to touch it until I said he could, mainly because I knew he was driving. He continued to drive and tell me how he'd been fantasizing about a guy he knows and wondered if he's gay. I suggested that he might be bisexual, which was my opinion and began to ask him questions about the guy. He told me that the other guy was a long time friend and he's been wanting to see his penis. When he fantasizes, he thinks of the friend sucking his penis in the car. *I wonder if the friend knows about this, and what would happen if he did.*

Talking about his friend really turned him on so I told him he'd better pull over. He pulled into a parking lot and continued talking about his friend. Then he changed tracks and said he'd love to show his penis to someone. There was a woman walking toward her car and he wanted desperately to show her. He wanted me to tell him to do it. *Sure, he gets in trouble and it's that "phone lady" again telling him to do bad things. I feel like I should be dressed in red with little horns and a pitchfork!* He was saying that she was by her car, putting groceries in the back and had no idea he was watching her with his penis out. .

Uh…let me think…No, he can't flash some innocent bystander. Next best thing. Fantasize about what she'd think if she saw his throbbing hard penis, how much she'd love to watch him stroke it and how it would make her horny. By this time, we'd gone over the fifteen minutes so I told him to imagine how she'd love watching him come all over his car and how he should do it now. He did. Close call. I thought for a minute he was really going to go up to the poor woman and give her quite a fright. After all, she could have had a cell phone to call a cop, mace, a pointed umbrella, or a 38! He was content to drive home after that.

#3—The Woods: He called again from the car but this time wanted to pull over and do something different. What now? One can only guess with this guy. He said he was coming up to a secluded area and was pulling over. Good idea, I thought. He said it was a wooded area, he parked his car and asked me, again, to "tell" him to strip. I figured it would be okay since he was in a private spot. It was about 6:30 am where he was, fall and the weather was crisp. I told him to take his pants off. He wanted to take his socks and shoes off too so I told him to do it. He asked if he should take his underwear off too. What the heck. Sure, take it off. He said he did. Then he asked if he should take off his shirt and tie. I told him he'd better not but he insisted that I needed to tell him to do it. Why waste time? Take off everything.

He says he's opening the car door to feel the cool air on his hard penis. He likes the word "penis." I heard the car door open and beeping noises like keys in the ignition or an alarm. Then I heard the door shut. He informed me that he was outside and wanted to walk around. I told him to get back in the car but he said he needed to walk. At first I wasn't really sure he was seriously outside, just like in the office, then heard the crunching of leaves. I could tell by his breathing and the noises that he was really outside, walking. Honestly, I can't ever imagine it being fun to be outdoors, naked, at 6:30 in the morning, in the woods on a cool fall day.

After a few minutes, he said he was at the edge of a wooded area looking into the parking lot of an apartment building. Here we go again! Just for a moment, get a mental picture of this. A fairly young, thirty something, business man with neatly trimmed brown hair and green eyes standing naked behind a tree at six thirty in the morning on a chilly day, with all of his clothing still in his car wearing only a big, hard penis. How nutty is that? It gets better.

He said he saw a couple in a car, talking and wanted to go up to them and show them his penis. This guy needs to take a picture of the darn thing and put it on the Internet. Then everyone can see it! I told him "NO." He should watch the people but stay behind the tree. I talked him through what it would be like if they both saw him stroking his beautiful penis as he was looking at them. How happy it would make them and how they'd want to have sex for hours after seeing him stroke himself. *I need high boots for all this crap I'm selling.* This seemed to do the trick and all of a sudden he said he came all over the ground. He took a deep breath, made a sigh of relief, and then realized where he was. Freaked out he said frantically "I can't believe the things I do when I get that horny!" It was like playing a record backwards. I heard him pant and run on the leaves, dinging of the door, shutting it and the ignition turned on. Said he was getting dressed and heading to the office. I sure hope he had a good day!

In The Store: This man said he wanted to go out in public with a huge hard on, letting it show. The first thing he asked me was what he should wear so everyone would notice especially the women. Not being summer, I suggested a pair of sweat pants with nothing underneath and a shorter tee shirt.

The first time we talked, it was all about wearing the sweat pants out to a department store and walking through the lady's department. He wanted to watch the pretty ladies shop while he played with himself right near them. He also wanted to take his penis out and walk by one of the women, brushing her with it. He'd say how he wanted to rub up against a pretty lady with a skirt on and put her hand on his penis. She would be so fascinated by it's beauty that she'd start to stroke it and tell him to mastur-bate right there in front of her. *Sure she would....* This was his first story. He was safe at home and just fantasizing about being out in public.

Next time he called, he was in his car and said he was wearing the sweat pants and on his way to the department store. I was skeptical until I heard the noises of a store. Now whether or not he was really wearing what he said, I don't know. I do think he was in the lady's department because I heard women talking here and there. He spotted a pretty woman in nice jeans and said he had his penis out under the clothing and was watching her. Then he said he wanted to go over and brush against her. At this point, I honestly didn't believe he had his penis out so I told him to go do it. I heard him say, "Oh, excuse me" to someone but no one replied. Now I'm really skeptical so I decided to play with him. I figured that if he really brushed a woman with his package exposed, she'd freak. If it's as big as he says it is, she'd surely notice, or someone else would, don't you think?

Now, throughout the entire conversation, which lasted a half-hour, he insisted that I tell him to do more daring things. After trying to talk him out of it and still not believing him I told him to go ahead, walk right up to her and show her his penis. "Really? Do you really think I should?" Now he was hesitant. I said, "Of course you should. Everyone wants to see your beautiful hard penis. Now go do it!" More of the, "Are you sure?" comments. I added one more thing. "Oh and you might want to look up and see where the cameras are located, because I'm sure you're being filmed right now." That did it, I think. He said he was still in the store, but I could tell by the noises that he went back to his car. He either got scared or I gave him his excuse for not doing it! *I think this gent was related to the one in the above three stories.*

I'm At The Doctor's Office: A frequent caller phoned me from his doctor's office. He was sitting in the exam room waiting for her to come in. I didn't ask why he was at the doctor. He said he was turned on and wanted to see if he could play with himself before she came in and not get caught.

He told me he could hear the people walking around outside the exam room and said he took his penis out of his pants. He asked me questions. "What do you think she'd say if she saw it? Do you think she wants to look at it? She'd like it, wouldn't she? Would my hard cock turn her on?" I told him he probably has the most beautiful cock in the world and I'm sure everyone would love to look at it. I'm sure it would turn his female doctor on so much that just looking at him would make her panties wet. What would she say if she came in and saw it? Well, she'd be so excited that she'd tell him how beautiful it is and how she just needs to look at it more.

He was pleased with this.....But I certainly hope he didn't take me seriously and whip it out for his doctor! I can just imagine him now telling the doctor, "But the phone sex lady said you'd like it!" Also, another case where I didn't believe the guy at first, until I heard the voices. In the background, not in my head.

Public Places—Reversed: This was the opposite. I was sitting in a restaurant with my cousin, male, and three of his friends, also male, when a call came in from a regular phone client. He liked to be dominated and spanked in front of people in his fantasies. In reality he was in the privacy of his own home.

I let him know I was out in public and he asked if I was sitting alone. I told him I was with three gentlemen and sitting in a corner booth. He asked if the restaurant was crowded. I told him that it was late and most people still there were at the bar area. He said he'd like to do the call with the people at the table listening. I'd ask everyone. They were more than eager to take part; so I called the client back and let everybody say hello to him.

I proceeded to take his call with all listening. The guy loved it, knowing that in a way he was in public with everyone at my table knowing what was going on. I made him talk loud and ask me for more spankings while holding the phone up so all at the table could hear. The client was satisfied and the guys at the table waited for me to hang up before they reacted. One chuckled, one just gasped and one laughed.

It was simply the idea that he was in public, yet completely anonymous that was such a turn on this time. I'm sure no one else heard, because I'm still welcome there!

FETISHES AND FANTASIES

This section is about specific fetishes. While many have a touch of domination, I'll save the serious S&M/domination fetishes for a later section. It's a book in itself! A sexual fetish is one that causes "habitual sexual response," according to the dictionary and is something to be devoted to. Sounds about right to me. Here are some of the fetishes I've encountered on the phone.

Feet & Shoes

I'd say that the most common is a foot fetish. Many have a favorite body part and consider themselves "leg" men, etc., but I mean a body part that they adore and are turned on by just looking at. I'm sure we all know someone who loves a woman's foot and would get totally turned on by nibbling or licking toes. My serious "foot fetish" clients go over the top with it however. Many subscribe to foot fetish magazines and own footsie porno's. One guy buys all sorts of ladies magazines, just so he can look at the feet. He loves Cosmo in the summer with all the beachy sandals and open toed shoes. Here's a sample of some of the "foot fetish" calls.

Feet Only: This guy had a serious foot fetish. Wanted a girlfriend who appreciated his love of feet and his desire to worship his ladies tootsies, but at this point in time, he didn't have anyone. So, he called me. I gave him the following fantasy and suggested that his next special lady should try it.

We're a dating couple, but instead of regular sex tonight, he wants to play a "foot only" game. He sits naked in a comfortable chair and I sit facing opposite him in just a pair of panties. He begins to stroke himself as I rub lotion on my feet and toes just to tease him. As he begins to get hard, I take one foot and slide it up his thigh, over his nipples and bring the foot up to his mouth.

When I got to this portion of the story, he was literally breathless, so I continued. He grabs my foot and starts to suck my toes and lick the underside of the foot. He gets even harder. I slide my lotioned foot over his hard penis and start stroking it. He sits back and lets me take over with both feet stoking him now. By this time, he'd stopped talking and just listened. I continue to play with him like this until he comes all over my pretty painted toes.

He called several times wanting the same story. Said he'd never fulfilled it but planned to. Hope his next girlfriend is up for the walk!

Worship my Feet: Guys with foot fantasies vary as much as with any other kind. This gentleman said he really enjoyed taking care of a woman's feet. His idea of a fun evening at home wasn't a typical dinner, movie, and/or sex. It's a "foot party" where he'd totally pamper the feet. I asked him what he'd like to do if I was there with him.

In this fantasy he'd be my boyfriend who worships my feet. He's prepared a footbath at his place, slips off my sandals and submerges my feet in warm, bubbly water while leisurely and gently washing them. After, he dries them with a fluffy heated towel and gives a gentle massage, all the while he's just looking and softly kissing them. I'm not so sure about the kissing part, but that heated towel and massage sounded really nice!

He paints my toenails pink and blows them dry with his warm breath. When they're dry, he rubs my feet against himself through his pants and instantly gets hard. This was a combination fantasy, his ideas and mine. Either way, he was ready for the sex part. He takes both feet and rubs them against his cheeks. *On his face, that is.* I tell him it's okay to rub them on his bare penis. Of course, he does so without hesitation. His hand is on one foot rubbing his penis, and the other is massaging his b's. He puts the towel on the floor and has me put my feet down. He begins stroking himself and I have to beg him to come all over my pretty pink toenails. I say this over and over again until he comes. He then licks my toes clean. *Hey, that was his idea.*

Tease Me Please: This gentleman likes to be teased before he is pleased. I conjured up this fantasy which he enjoyed immensely.

He is lying back on some big pillows. I sit next to him, slowly take off my shoes and run my foot up and down his pant leg. I rest my leg on his lap and begin to sensually slip off a thigh high stocking. I do the same thing with the other leg. He reaches for my foot and I tell him, "No…Not yet. Rest your hands behind your head please." He does. I take the stocking and run it across his face and bare chest, under his nose and over his lips. He is becoming excited. I do the same thing with my foot now, running it over his face, caressing his lips with my toes. He is squirming now, but I still won't let him touch yet. This goes on until I give him permission to touch my feet. From there, he is allowed to lick, suck and caress them. It goes from there into great sex with him holding on to my feet. *As I'm talking, I'm trying to figure out what positions people could get into to accomplish the foot holding. There are a few I guess*

Heel To Toe: This guy loves shoes…Likes feet, but loves shoes. Leather and patent leather. Says the feel; smell and taste drive him wild. Now that's all he really told me about what he wanted so I figured it was time to be a bit creative. I thought this up and went with it even though it was a little different. Turned out well.

He comes to my place, which is all set up for him. I tell him to sit comfortably on the love seat. In front of him is an oversized coffee table made of wood and very shiny. Large candles are placed around the room for light and a bottle of wine next to him on the end table. "This is going to be a nice evening," I tell him. "Just the way you like it." *Notice that I always have a bottle of wine available? That's my idea!*

I'm dressed in a black lace bra & thong with matching garter belt and thigh high stockings, lace trimmed with a seam up the back. I'm not wearing any shoes yet. He pours the wine while I go over to a small lamp and turn it on. On the soft carpet are four pairs of shoes. Two leather, two patent leather. All have four or five inch heels and closed toes. I take the first black pair and bring it over to him. They are patent leather with a delicate rhinestone strap across the ankle. Very elegant. I brush them just under his nose and tell him to take a sniff. He does and sighs. I put them on in front of him. The next pair is red. Leather. Five-inch heels, closed toe and open heel with a lace up tie. He smells them and I put them in his lap. He begins to get turned on.

Next are the black patent leather platforms, sexy and a little trashy. I let him have a quick lick and place them next to him on the table. I bring a beautiful, sexy gold pair of leather heels over to him that I've worn all day. He gets visibly turned on, sniffs them and I put them up against his thigh.

He takes out his penis and starts stroking himself while I rub the shoes up and down the shaft of his hard cock. Then one by one, each shoe is brought under his nose to smell and lick. All the while I'm emphasizing the feel, scent and sound of the shoe material.

As I described this fantasy, he never made it to the last shoe. I think he came somewhere around five. Next time I'll tell him it's only three pairs.

Lick My Shoes: Another shoe guy. Young, mid twenties and the feel and smell of worn, women's shoes drives him out of his mind. For one of his fantasies, I told him that I'd let him in to the dressing room at a strip bar and leave him alone. He'd go from shoe to shoe, smelling each one and deciding which scent he liked best. Then he'd start to lick the shoes, outside and in. Red ones, black ones, white ones, shiny ones, boots and sandals.

He was quite excited already. I could tell because he was panting! So I told him that he'd be unable to contain himself anymore and would just have to play a little back there. He'd enjoy masturbating while licking and sniffing his favorite pair of heels. Later he would see a girl wearing the shoes he liked best making his experience even more enjoyable.

Note: I knew a young gentleman that was having me analyze his handwriting. He had to write a line or two for a mini analysis and sign his name. He wrote, "I want to lick and suck your toes." I could tell by his writing that he was serious!

Panty Fetishes

Being female, I don't understand the desire to play with, smell and/or lick worn underwear, but many and I mean many men love it. Come on you guys....how many times have you been at a strip bar and put the panties over your head. Don't lie now, I've seen it and don't blame the booze. I've also given out and sold plenty of my own. Even had a few pairs stolen from bachelor parties. Guess it's an animal instinct and that's about it. I have a male dog, who is a panty thief. If he gets a pair he'll carry them around with him wherever he goes. See what I mean?

So, through the course of these conversations men have requested underwear. My questions to them are, "Do you want them straight out of the panty drawer, or straight off of me?" You can guess that no one ever requested the undies out of the drawer. I'll send out panties to clients and in turn, they usually call me when they receive them, wanting a sex call.

I Want Your Panties: A guy who called quite often requested a pair of worn panties. Ad I said before, not that unusual in this business. Sent him the undies at the regular charge and he said he'd call on the day he received them. The charge at the time was around $14.95 for a non brand name.

He called to say he'd received the package and was ready to open it. As we spoke, he unwrapped his parcel and described everything. The little personal note I put in, to the wrapping, to the plastic bag to the panty. He detailed exactly what he was doing with the underwear. Looking at them, smelling each part and on to licking them. On to rubbing the panties over his naked body, to masturbating with the panties wrapped around his penis. He fantasized that I was there with him and he'd taken them off personally. He won't come on the panties though as he wants to use them again and he does, on every call.

People have asked how I feel knowing guys have my underwear. Well, it was weird at first but like anything else, you get used to it.

Panty Requests: Here are the most requested panties themes:
*They must be worn.
*They want the girl to rub herself while talking to them and send those panties.
*Rub the thong in between the cheeks of the butt.
*Masturbate in them.
*Come in them.
*Have sex in them.
*Pee in them (more popular than you'd imagine)
*Send them with pubic hair.

Odder Requests::

*One guy wanted a pair worn for three days! I told him that overnight was the best I could do. *How gross.*
*Send them with poop. *Yuk! Even more disgusting!*
*Have sex in them and have the guy come on them. *Strange.*
*Once and only once, a guy requested menstrual blood. *OK, that's more than just "out there," it's just plain sick.*

Although I have sent worn panties to clients, I won't fill the odd requests. Weren't we taught as kiddies NOT to poop in our underwear? Don't get me wrong, if someone actually wants to pay for soiled or sex stained underwear, that's their business and if someone can make money with it, have a ball. I just can't handle it personally.

Men In Panties—Some With Dildos:

There are so many men who not only want the panties we women wear, but as I mentioned earlier, like to wear ladies lingerie also. Panties are the favorite. Stockings, pantyhose, garter belts and bras are next in line and some like to finish things with a nightie and/or robe. Teddies are in there too. Although there are plenty of mens satin and silk underwear in thong, g-string and bikini styles, many want to wear actual women's underwear. This topic goes much further into complete cross dressing, but I'm talking about those guys who just like the panty thing right now.

While many who wear panties are completely heterosexual, more than half do like anal sex and/or have "toys" of their own. Some have bisexual fantasies, others don't. I've had many ask if I think they're gay. I simply ask them a few questions. For example, have any of them had girlfriends who like anal sex? Most answer that some did and others didn't. In my opinion, that is simply another body part that some people find erotic and others do not. Whether one is male of female, what's the difference? Then I ask them if they would like their significant other to use a dildo or vibrator on them, or would they like a man to have sex with them. If they answer "no" to a man, then I tell them I believe they are straight. If they answer "yes," the answer is obvious. So what? Be who you are. I find many times that they are relieved to hear that plenty more men feel the same. Here are a few interesting stories.

Look At Me! One man called to tell me that he loved to wear panties and wanted to send pictures. I told him he could e-mail me a photo. He took the picture himself in a mirror, which was a body shot only and wore nothing but see through cream-colored bikini panties. He was dark and hairy and sent both a front and rear shot. *I must say he had a nicely rounded tush.*

His phone call was mostly talk about the times he wore panties in front of ladies. One time he was at a swimming pool at a hotel on vacation. He took off his clothing down to his bathing suit like everyone else, except that he was wearing panties instead. It turned him on to see the reactions. He said that some looked surprised, others giggled, some stared and a little old lady looked away.

On another occasion, he enjoyed changing into different panties and modeling them in front of his mirror, which was, coincidentally, next to a window. Wouldn't you know it? His shades were up and the lights on, so that the people in the other apartments could see in. He loved the thought of not knowing who was watching.

On still another occasion, he said went to see a costume lady who worked with strippers. He wanted custom made panties. She fitted him and let him try on different things. She apparently liked playing dress up with him and let him talk about himself in his panties. That's his favorite thing in the world! I don't know whether he had some made or not but he enjoyed the "fashion show" he says.

Each time he calls, he just likes to talk about these things and it turns him on. I sent him a pair of my undies about two years ago and he still has them. They were a pair of very stretchy lace thongs, which he says he wears. *Ouch…they have to be tight.*

Come And Get Me: A very personable man calls from time to time who is as heterosexual as can be, but loves to wear panties. At first he was into panties only. After a year and a half, he's now enjoying bras and thigh-highs. He tells me all about ladies he dates and seems like a nice guy who does the flowers and candy thing. When he calls me, he's in a different frame of mind. He's in a dress up mood and enjoys being called names, like, "little slut," "nasty little bitch" and "dirty whore."

He likes to prop his feet on a table facing a mirror and watch himself play while wearing the pretty underwear. We go through what it would be like if I was standing next to or in front of him, telling him what a little bitch he is and how he looks like a slut. I tell him I'm going to treat him like the slut he is, strap on a big dildo and screw the hell out of him. He's told to pull his panties to the side and wait for the big dildo that he's going to get hard and fast. He also says naughty things like, "Fuck me in my panties," or, "I'm a little bitch whore." I instruct him to play with himself and ask my permission to come. When he's finished, we'll chat about football or something else "normal" and that's that.

The Nurse with the Strap On: Yup, you read it right. When this guy first called and I asked him what he liked, he said he wanted me to be a naughty nurse. I automatically thought about the typical naughty nurse who seduces her patient. Not sure, I asked, "And just what would this naughty nurse be doing?" He said the nurse would have a dildo with her. Now I knew what he wanted. So here's how it went.

In this fantasy, I come into the room to give him an exam. He wants to be checked all over. After I check him, I tell him he needs to be shaved, which makes him very hard. I got an, "mmmmm"….out of him when I mentioned the shaving so I figured I was on the right track. I rub lotion all over his penis and b's and in between his cheeks afterward. Then he asks me what I have over there on the table. I tell him it's my strap on dildo and that I want him to take it. *I've never heard of a nurse carrying around a big dildo for the patients, but this IS a fantasy you know. They don't always make sense.* I take my uniform off, strap on this ten-inch dildo and give it to him real good. I make him watch me and play with himself. He comes, I go.

The Dildo Saleslady: This is a good story. I don't know much about this guy, except that he's middle aged and professional. He uses a girly name when he calls, although he has a truly deep voice, which he doesn't at all try to disguise. He likes to cross dress and use a dildo.

On one call he asked me to tell him a story. He set it up and I took it from there. I was "Lola," the dildo saleslady who he was expecting to visit. His name was "Lilly." When I arrived, he was wearing all black; a black patent leather, lace up corset with eight garters attaching black silk stockings seamed up the back. Add to that a black cone shaped bra, sheer silk bikini panties, long black gloves and black patent leather heels. Not just heels though. These would be nine-inch heels with a four-inch platform. His hair and makeup would be perfect, dark and sultry and he would be wearing a long, sheer, black robe. This is as far as he would take it. I had to improvise the rest and believe me, when you're on the phone for a minimum of forty-five minutes of story telling it's not as easy as you might think. My turn to take over.

He said he'd like Lola to be wearing a corset also so this is what I decided on. All red. A short, red leather miniskirt with a matching jacket, thigh high boots with a six-inch heel and two-inch platform. Black silk stockings are barely peeking out above the boots and are lace topped. He loves details. Can you tell?

When Lola enters the room, Lilly takes off her jacket. She's wearing a red patent leather corset; tight and laced up to make an already tiny waist look even smaller. Lola has on red gloves that go all the way up the arm, with a diamond bracelet over the wrist and a matching necklace. She asks Lilly if the skirt should be removed. Yes. Underneath, Lola's corset has four garters, which attach to her stockings. Her red thong panty is very see through and a built in bra pushes her breasts up and out showing a full cleavage.

Lola sits comfortably on a chair and puts her briefcase on a table. Lilly sits relaxing on the sofa while Lola begins to show her/him an assortment of dildos. The dildo parade starts with some little ones and graduates to more realistic looking, larger ones. Lilly is just fascinated and is getting turned on just by looking and touching them.

This guy knows a LOT about dildos. I don't know if he looks at catalogues or goes to adult stores but he is schooled in the many varieties, shapes, sizes, colors and functions of dildos. I didn't know much, so I'd ask him questions. "So tell me about that new dildo you bought," or "Oh really? I want to know all about that one." He'd give descriptions and help me along a little without really trying. The story goes on.

Lola reaches into her bag and pulls out a "special" dildo that is for "special" customers only. It's a twelve-inch long, two and a half-inch around, red dildo, complete with a set of balls attached. The gentleman actually did describe this particular dildo as being the one he uses when he calls me….his favorite. Lilly gasps with delight. Lola slowly takes it out of the package and hands it to her/him. He feels and caresses it, putting it to his face and licking it a few times.

Lola asks for some warm water. When Lilly returns with it, Lola has put some lubricating gel inside the balls of the dildo. Add warm water and it's ready to go. Lilly just has to have this dildo, so Lola offers to let Lilly try it out, right then and there. Lola tells Lilly to lie back and take the panties off. Lilly announces that her/his butthole is flaming hot just like a pussy and is ready for all twelve inches. *This is actually what he says on the phone.*

Lola proceeds to give Lilly what she/he wants, slowly at first, until she/he can take the whole thing. Then Lola just rams that twelve inches like crazy, telling Lilly to "come like a girl." When Lilly is ready, Lola shoots the warm liquid into Lilly's butt. Lilly gives a happy sigh of relief and of course buys the dildo. Lola gets her skirt and jacket back on, tucks her dildos into the case and says goodbye, promising to come back again soon.

Now let me remind you, this is the short version of this story. I had to play it out for nearly an hour, putting in lots of details as we went along. The caller was quite happy and called on more than a few occasions.

I honestly believe he really does wear the outfits he describes to me and has a twelve-inch, red dildo. Once, he had to get something in another room, put the phone down and I heard those platforms clunking all the way back and forth. Also, his descriptions are pretty much the same with a change of outfit now and then. He's even told me the catalogues he gets his corsets from. After all this time, I can tell whether it's just fantasy or not. I don't think this one is. Well, it doesn't really matter anyway, as long as he's a happy client having fun and I'm a happy phone sex lady getting paid.

The Double Dildo: This man has called about seven or eight times, always with the same fantasy. He is wearing sheer panties in feminine colors like pink, white or cream and a matching bra. I too am in lingerie of my choice. We sit facing each other and have "girl talk" for a while. Then he reaches under the bed and pulls out a double-headed dildo about twenty inches in length all totaled. I, of course, am amazed and can't wait to try it. *Now that's pushing it...no pun intended.* He pulls his panties down and exposes a big hard-on. I take mine off also and we begin to play with the dildo. We play together and push on it. The object is to meet in the middle. I tell him that I can only take eight inches, which means he has to take twelve to reach me. He struggles, but takes it all, and loves it. We ride the big dildo together until we both come wildly. What can I say? He likes it!

Some "confessions" to Marie that they don't want anyone to know:

*They really want to buy a dildo.

*They've already bought a dildo.

*They have a collection of dildos.

*They'd love for their girl to use one on them but won't ask.

*They are fantasizing that the dildo is really a guy.

Little Penis

There are actually many men who like women to humiliate and make fun of their small penis size. Maybe some have low self-esteem about the situation and deal with it by making fun of themselves and maybe others really like to be humiliated. Personally, I wouldn't make fun of a man with a tiny penis. It's not his doing. After all, do women want to criticized because of what they think of as flaws? Of course not. Now, do women WANT an exceptionally small penis? I highly doubt it, which is probably where these calls stem from.

Some of the following fantasies are a bit different, to say the least. They include voyeurism, humiliation, cross-dressing and threesomes. Some of the stuff might make you squirm and say "eeeeww", but that's how it is.

Let Me Watch…Laugh At My Penis: This man claims his stories to be true, but I have serious doubts. If they are true, then he really needs help with his self-image. Here goes. He professes to enjoy watching his wife have sex with other men, while he's made to sit in a chair and watch. The other man and the wife laugh at the husbands' small penis. She tells him how he can't please her with such a little one and that she can't even feel it when they have sex.

Both the husband and wife are Caucasian and the other man is black. Seems popular, doesn't it? He shows the husband his large penis and says that he will please the man's wife. She instructs her husband to play with his little cock and watch. The big, black man has wild sex with the wife and when he's about to come, tells the wife that he's going to make her pregnant. *He came up with this out of no where.* He comes inside her with a force. Now it might get a little offensive to some: The husband, my phone client, must lick her clean until there's none left. In his fantasy, or reality as he tells it, this will continue until the wife gets pregnant. He called about four or five times. *For the record, I had NO part in that.*

After approximately a six-month absence, he called back, starting from the beginning. He said he'd taken some half-naked pictures of his wife and placed them in the mens room at his office for all to see. When he was sure one of his co-workers was interested, he told the guy that it would be okay to take his wife out on a date. They started going out on dates and when she came home, the husband would look to see if she was mussed up at all, hoping that there had been some sexual action. He actually called to let me know that his wife had been out on about four dates and said they hadn't had sex yet. The client was disappointed.

Then one night, he called to say that she'd gone out again with the man from work and came home all tousled, makeup smeared and her blouse partially unbuttoned. When asked how it went, she pulled her panties out of her purse and gave them to her husband. *It gets gross again.* He sucked on the panties and then lifted her skirt to "clean her up." I haven't heard from him in a while. Maybe she had twins?

See My Little Peepee? You'd think most guys would want to e-mail me pictures of their larger than average penises, but not this one. He was proud to have an "almost" four-inch penis and liked to be teased with no mercy. He asked if he could send pictures for me to look at while we talked. I don't know why, but I agreed and he certainly did send them, one with a ruler on it. Yup, almost four inches all right. From the rather close up picture, he looked overweight, so he'd probably measure bigger if he were thinner. He wanted me to talk about his small size and tell him how I'd never be happy with such a little one. It's even too small to be called a penis. Instead, we'd call it a little peepee.

I told him he doesn't deserve a woman and all he could do was play with it by himself while I showed his pictures to all my friends. We would all laugh at him. This really turned him on! He'd asked how many friends were laughing at him. I informed him that I told everyone and would proceed to name girls and sometimes give descriptions of some. At the end of the call, he'd give me a simple, "Thank you that was fun" and politely say goodbye. He called a few times and seemed quite satisfied. I did delete the photos though.

Three Inches And A Porn Booth: This guy called regularly and at just about the time I thought he was really nuts, he told me that all of his stories were 90 percent fantasy. The true parts: He apparently has a three-inch penis, almost four when erect. He likes to be made fun of because of his size and always asks me whom I've told about him. I'd say that I told different guys and gals and he was delighted. The more the better. He wanted to know what their reactions were. Anything from a gasp, to a giggle, a jolly laugh, to a word of sympathy.

The not so true part: He said he visits adult stores often that have back rooms where a guy can "stick it through a hole and get it sucked." Says he goes to these places and just services men, as many as he can find. He takes about four or five "loads" in his mouth and then lets as many as possible screw him in the ass. He said he also licks everyone else's ass after they've been screwed. *See why I was concerned? A disease waiting to happen.*

He said he frequents places where men watch a girl from behind glass while masturbating, so of course, he licks the glass and floor clean. He'd tell me he'd visited four or five bookstores in one day and enjoyed talking about the ladies who worked in the stores laughing at him and his little penis. He tells me that he calls me upon his return home.

His calls are always similar, relating his adventures at the porn booths. He's got to be one of the friendliest guys I've ever spoken to. I hope that his lack of penis size doesn't mess with his self-esteem in his non-fantasy world.

My Wife Laughs At Me: Another guy with "four inches at best" called with similar situations to the ones mentioned previously. He too was married and claimed he couldn't please his wife because he was so small. Come on now, most people would have a clue ahead of time. Wouldn't you think she'd know if he could please her or not before the I Do's?

All that aside, he said she'd laugh at him or would tell him to get away from her. He thought she might be having an affair with another man. Just as I was starting to feel sorry for the guy, he let on that it really turns him on when she laughs at him and tells him to go play with himself. Said he'd play with it while they were laying in bed at night with her facing in the other direction. Sometimes she'd ask him if he was using his two fingers for that little weenie. He'd have to come on himself while she just fell asleep. I'm not sure his story is real, but he was happy and I got paid.

It's Not Little Enough: Same guy. He called back one time in particular to tell me he was disappointed because he'd heard that there were men with even smaller penises than his. I don't get it. Was this guy trying to get into the book of records for the smallest package? Anyway, he searched the Internet and found guys with littler peepees than his. He said he found some that were two and three inches and suggested I check out the website while we were on the phone, which I did. He was right, and although I'm no expert, I don't think the photos were computer enhanced. These really were some tiny dudes! As for the call, he continued to talk about his little peepee and that would turn him on. A little different, yes. How many guys would be upset to find out that they don't have the world's record for the "Smallest Penis?"

Naughty Boy!

Let's get into some discipline. There are guys who enjoy being told what to do, spanked, bossed around and more. We're not talking about a slap on the rear. It's a good ass whippin' and a fantasy to go along with it. Personally, I get a kick out of these. Here are a few samples:

A Public Spanking: This client loves the idea of being spanked in public. He likes to come up with the idea and we work together throughout his fantasy. He also has a foot fetish, which we work in and wants me to be the authority figure, so in many of his stories I'm his step-mom.

He's a college student who's pampered by his dad and the step mom is tired of it. Step mom gets a call from the school about the young man being caught sneaking into the ladies locker room and stealing panties. She tells the bad boy that dad will be told and he'll certainly cut his money off, or he can face her punishment. He chooses the punishment.

His step mom brings him to the school and into the classroom our bad boy. In the room are the teacher and the five girls whose panties he's taken. They are all in sandals and skirts or shorts. *That's where we work in the foot fetish.* The teacher has a long, sheer, flowy skirt with hippie type sandals, an ankle bracelet and toe ring.

Step mom puts a chair in front of the class and begins talking to the girls while the "bad boy" stands facing them. She will be spanking him in front of everyone and embarrass him just as he's embarrassed them. One girl laughs, the other giggles, one is shy and red faced and the other two are just shocked. Oh yes, his girlfriend is always one of the girls present. She is mad at him for stealing other women's underwear!

The teacher is sitting down and step mom instructs the bad boy to bend over her knee. He objects but does it anyway. All the girls are giggling now. He looks so silly over mommy's knee. She gives him one or two smacks on the butt and has him stand up, take his shoes off and bend over again. She orders the bad boy to look at everyone's feet, knowing full well that this will turn him on. He'll really be embarrassed with a hard on. She takes a hairbrush and smacks his rear end again, then has him stand up and face the class. She quickly yanks his pants down to show his tidy white underwear. He's now standing there in front of five girls and a teacher in his white undies with a big hard on. Can you just picture this?

He goes back over her knee and step mom holds his underwear down under his butt while the teacher spanks him. He must repeat out loud: "Bad boys get bare bottom spankings." This goes on until the end….when he's finished on the phone, that is.

This client always says, "Thank you, that was great!" He's polite and seems to be nice. Wonder if he really gets into the spanking thing.

"I'm Sorry, Sister Marie": This guy has the same public spanking type fantasy with an even stronger authority figure….the nun. Hey, anyone can pretend to be a nun, right? Sister Marie for this one.

The bad schoolboy is taken to Sister Marie's office. A sweet, young nun brings him, terribly shy and embarrassed. She tells Sister Marie that the bad boy has been talking dirty to the girls in class again. "You've been to my office three times this week for the same thing and looking at your record, you were here two times before this for looking up their skirts. What do you have to say for yourself?" "I don't know Sister Marie. I just can't help it sometimes. I'm sorry. I won't do it again." Sister Marie doesn't believe him and decides he must be punished. The shy young nun prepares to leave the room but is called back to observe. She obediently sits. The bad boy is told to come to Sister's desk and bend over. He protests, but Sister Marie snaps a ruler on the edge of the chair, making both of them jump. He does as told.

His pants are pulled down but before he is spanked, Sister Marie puts the intercom on. Now everyone can all hear what's going on. The Sister spanks the bad boy with the ruler, making him count to twenty. Then she spanks him with a paddle while he counts again. Finally, she takes a belt to his rear end and once more makes him count. Now that he is totally humiliated, he must return to the class with the shy nun and apologize to the girls. They all giggle, the nun is red faced, Sister Marie had fun and the bad boy said "thank you" before he hung up.

Another frequent flyer on the phone. He calls often with these types of fantasies, but I don't think he carries them over into real life. Maybe he should. It would cost less.

Finger Licking Good…(or Bad): This guy calls often but struggles with himself about it. He feels he shouldn't but does anyway. Maybe it's because the things that arouse him would be on the repulsive side to most. My feeling on it? I tell him not to feel badly about calling. After all, he's harming no one except himself maybe, as you'll read. *This one can get kind of nasty but I'm used to it by now and you probably are too.*

He'll call and say he's being a bad boy. In our earlier conversations he'd say he was playing with himself or watching a porno. In the later conversations, he'd say he was sticking his fingers up his butt and/or playing with a dildo. I took this as a clue to be more aggressive. He wanted to do anything to please me, from a bath to sexual pleasure, to servicing all my friends, male and female. Even licking their butts and drinking their pee was a go. Yes, he does mean anything! Here's a sample of the finger licker.

He is instructed to use each finger, one at a time and "pump" his rear end five times with each. Then I make him lick them. *He could be licking a lollipop on the phone for all I know.* He says it tastes good. Since he's been a bad boy with his dirty fingers he'd have to give all my friends a butt-licking bath and must describe how he'd lick them all. Then he has to service their boyfriends, giving them oral sex and sometimes taking care of four at once. He must drink pee from everyone there, starting with the females and then the males. He also must lick a dirty rear end and be peed on. This would prove how loyal he is to me. Once in a while I make him play with his dildo and when he's all turned on, he has to wait to come.

His voice then goes back to a deeper tone, he says thank you, tells me to have a nice day and hangs up. He always sounds embarrassed. I think he needs to surf the Internet and see just how many others there are like him. Then he wouldn't feel so bad.

Don't Use That Word!: Now this was a serious caller. He knew what he liked and expected perfection. Our first phone encounter was an hour long just talking about how he wanted his future calls to go. He asked me to actually take notes. He explained that he doesn't have sex in real life partially due to his sexual background, which he'd get into at a later time. He masturbates. That's it.

He did go into a little, saying that as a teen, his sister and her more aggressive friend caught him masturbating. He liked that. Eventually they'd make him do it in front of them and watch, sometimes forcing him to wear panties and stockings. Very peculiar, especially if he was being truthful. Who knows? He's also mentioned that there's more to the story and would tell me someday. I'm not sure I want to know.

He had an actual script of expressions for me to say, over and over, word for word. Things like, "All I want you to do is lay in your bed and masturbate." "You like to masturbate, don't you?" "Just lay there and masturbate your little cock for me." "I'm going to teach you to ejaculate on command." "I'm going to drain every drop of sperm from your tiny dick." I had a list of about twenty sentences like that and would have to repeat them. Before I could get into these sentences, I had to tell him to look briefly at pictures of naked girls on his wall. He said it wasn't a big turn on but allright for a beginning. Then we could get into the main part of his call.

His one turn off? I could not under any circumstances, use the word "come." He hated that word and if it was used accidentally, he'd literally count the number of times it was said. One of the things he was looking for in a phone sex partner was someone who handled his calls perfectly and never used that word! He made sure to point out the two times I slipped on the first call we actually did. A forgivable offense, since I was new with him.

Once we got through all his sentences, I was told to watch the clock for a "ejaculation countdown." Even that had to be perfect! It would start at two minutes when I'd tell him it was his "two minute countdown." Then, silence for a minute until I'd tell him it was his "sixty second countdown." Silence, until "thirty seconds," "fifteen seconds," and finally the big finale of "five, four, three, two....now!" The words in the countdown had to be exact also. He'd make all sorts of loud noises and while he was making them I had to tell him to "soak your bed sheets with sperm" and "wipe yourself with your bed sheets." That's how it went.

If this wasn't difficult enough, he'd call only after 2:00 am. Try to concentrate on this type of a call when you're half-asleep! This put limits on the amount of calls I've done with him. Even with his odd fetish, he was polite and courteous. I hope that whatever sexual issues he has from his past get resolved at some time.

The Mean Step Auntie: This gentleman called on a regular basis for quite some time. He said he was a single, white-collar worker who dated regularly. He was as "normal" as the next guy from what I gathered, just had fantasies about being spanked and made to take a dildo.

Here are two of the many fantasies we've explored. In all cases, he was the "naughty nephew" who was a bad young man in great need of discipline. He's taken advantage of auntie's generosity, used auntie's credit cards for porno, smoked pot in the house and never does his chores. ('Cause he's always stoned and watching porns)

#1: The Party: Auntie just received a huge bill on her credit card showing rented porno videos all month long. Only the naughty nephew has access to her cards. What should auntie do?

I know. His boss is a good friend of mine; I'd be able to get him fired from his great job in an instant. He loves the good pay and the boss's daughter. She just accepted a lunch date with the naughty nephew and he doesn't want to be fired now. Auntie has also said she'd reveal to the boss ad her daughter that he rents pornos all the time, including those featuring gay males. Naughty nephew is worried now and knows that auntie has proof right in her hands. To make things worse, when auntie confronts her bad boy nephew, he's not only watching the porno's, but also wearing her bra and panties!

Auntie gives him an ultimatum. Do what I say and take the punishment or else. He would do what I asked. So, I'd dress him up in a French Maid outfit and invite a bunch of girlfriends over for a naughty nightie party. He must be our server. During the party, I'd tell my friends what a bad boy he'd been and how he needs some punishment. I even show them how he's stretched out my beautiful underwear, which is SO expensive. They all agree so I make him lie on the coffee table, pull up his little ruffled skirt and spank him with a paddle in front of everyone. He complains, so I give the paddle to everyone in the room who then take turns spanking him also. He has to count out loud to twenty each time he's spanked. Which he does on the phone.

I make him stay in that position while we bring out dildos to go along with the sexy nighties. We decide a demonstration is needed and we'll use the naughty nephew. He pleads for us not to, but he has to take his punishment. Down come the little panties and in goes the dildo. We make him say, "fuck me with the dildo," over and over again until we decide he's had enough. He has to promise to be a good boy before we stop.

#2: The Rock Show: Auntie gives her nephew a great opportunity. She has tickets and back stage passes to a show featuring his favorite rock band. All she asks him to do is clean up the house while she's at work. When she comes home, she finds him sleeping on the sofa, smelling of pot, along with the rest of the house, which is not picked up at all. There are dishes in the sink and beer cans all around, so he must have had his friends over. Auntie is furious and tells him he can't go at all. He begs, pleads and even cries.

Now, auntie has a selfish streak and knows a member or two from the band. She knows what they like and decides to use it to her advantage. She tells the nephew to get dressed, and wear a bra and panties under his clothes. He does what she says. They go to the concert, have a good time and go back stage as promised. Nephew is stopped at the stage door and handed another outfit by anutie. It's a little schoolgirl skirt and blouse with knee socks and buckle shoes. He's told to go change or he can't come back stage. He obeys and is then allowed in the room where he's the only one dressed like this. Everyone there is looking at him and they are heard saying, "This must be our entertainment." Nephew is sweating now. He has an idea what's coming.

He's made to get on his knees and give oral sex to the guys in the room. He's then bent over, spanked with a dildo and made to have sex with one of the men while he sucks the other one. At the end, everyone gives him a round of applause and he gets to meet the band members. *This one was actually his entire idea.*

One thing I've notice about these fantasies is that the guys are almost always imagining a situation where they're forced into sexual situation. Seems to be a common thread. Maybe it's their way of being able to accept the fact they fantasize about men.

Really Different Fetishes—Some Nasty Ones:

So far we've covered numerous types of fetishes and although some may seem eccentric, they get even more bizarre. The next group is the milder of the oddities, but enough so you'll get an idea what goes on in some people's minds. I've left out the people who have requested severe torture and beatings. We definitely won't go into the few that have requested castration! *Yeah, there have been some.* We'll now enter the world of the strange fetishes.

Little Sissy Baby: A professional gentleman who likes to be dominated. Why isn't this story in the "domination" section? Because he has a diaper fetish which to me, seems odd. He likes to be called names like "little sissy boy" and "bad little diaper boy" while pretending to be a grown up baby. He refers to himself as grown while acting like a little baby. Honestly, I have no idea if he's really wearing diapers or not. I think if he wore them while on the phone, I'd hear "diaper noises." So I'll assume it's fantasy. Here's one of his typical stories:

He calls to say he's being a bad boy and is playing with his wee-wee which is getting hard. Then he tells me some of the things his "mommie mistress" makes him do, who in reality, he claims is his girlfriend. He has to "suck her panties, lick her pussy and smell her ass," while wearing a diaper. He has to be a good boy and not pee in the diaper.

When he calls me, he wants to know if I'd diaper him in front of my girlfriends. I tell him that everyone is going to watch his little wee-wee while we diaper him, powder his rear end and put baby oil on him. Of course we have a bad girl in the group who likes to show the little sissy boy her panties and let him smell them. This makes his little wee wee hard and he reaches into his diaper to play with it. Then he's allowed to sit with his diaper undone and play with himself in front of the girls until he "squirts" everywhere like a big boy. *The uses of the expressive words are his idea.*

He not at all embarrassed about his fetish. Says he has a job with huge responsibilities and this is his way of escaping. A glass of champagne and a hot tub would do it for me, but different strokes.

Tickle & Tie Me: Yes, he liked to be tickled while tied up. I know nothing about this caller except for his fantasies. Didn't tell me anything about himself. Here's how it goes. He wants to be tied to a bed, hands and feet and be seriously tickled. I told him I'd tickle him with feathers, scarves and the silk stockings to start. He wanted more, like fingers in the ribs. OK, so we don't want sensual tickling here. I said I'd get on top of him and roughly tickle his ribs, kneecaps, thighs and groin. That turned him on. Go figure.

At times he'd be blindfolded and have his penis stroked with one hand while being tickled with the other. This would go back and forth until I felt he'd had enough. I'd untie one hand and let him masturbate. He only called a few times. Maybe he found someone rougher.

Smoke Anyone? Ever heard of a smoking fetish, combined with bondage? Me either, until now. This man wanted to be tied to a table, preferably a medical table and slowly have every sense taken away from him. *I think there are more than two fetishes going on here, don't you?*

I'd be wearing something black, leather or patent leather and have two assistants who were not in the room yet. He would be tied with big leather straps, buckled around his waist, chest, thighs and arms. There would be smaller straps around his wrists, ankles, elbows and knees. I asked him how that would feel. He said he felt somewhat restrained. The word "somewhat" made me figure he wanted more.

Gloves would be put on his hands so he couldn't rub his fingers together, more straps going up his legs and arms, one around his neck, forehead and numerous straps up and down his body so that he couldn't move at all. Now he said he felt restrained.

I don't know about you, but that alone would make me insane. He wanted more. He would then be blindfolded with leather so there was absolutely NO light. He'd only be able to hear. Then I'd open a door so he could hear footsteps of two people and male voices. To his left someone is banging something against a counter, like cigarettes being packed down. As we talk, he hears something crackling, like plastic wrapping. A match is struck and he wonders if we're going to burn him. Then he smells a cigarette. I take a puff and blow smoke in his face. He coughs. I tell him to breathe it in next time and do it again. He does as told.

He then feels someone's hand on his pants, unzipping him and pulling his penis out to be exposed. It isn't me as I'm by his ear, talking to him. While my assistant is doing this, the other one lights another cigarette and hands it to me. I tell the client that this time he has to take a long puff and hold it until I say he can release it. Then I make him do it. I tell him to hold it for sixty seconds but he releases it too soon and begins to cough. Now has to do it again, but for ninety seconds. I make him take a very long puff and my assistant puts a gag in his mouth. I sit by his head, count to ninety and release the gag.

He's done as instructed, although by force and is allowed to be "stroked" by the assistant until he is relieved. He actually does smoke and hold it in on the phone but most times he really can't hold it as long as I tell him to. Told you it was uncommon.

You Need Your Temperature Checked: Medical examination fantasies. Some really enjoy this. Personally, I stay as far away from medical procedures as possible but not this guy. Said he was in his early forties, average looking and slender. He wanted to be in a hospital room and in need of a rectal exam by a nurse. He had a thing for medical rooms and anal sex. Let's combine the two.

The room is white, with the patient sitting in his hospital bed, wearing a little blue and white hospital gown. He looks so vulnerable.

In walks a sexy nurse. *Aren't the nurses always sexy?* She tells the patient that he needs to be checked and have his temperature taken. He opens his mouth but she says she'll take it rectally. "Now, just turn over like a good boy and it will be over shortly." He does as the nurse says. She lubes up the thermometer and puts it in his butt, moving it around and telling him she's trying to read it. Since his pants are off she notices he is getting hard. Being a "bad" nurse, she takes advantage of it. Pulling the thermometer out, she tells him, "No temperature, but stay right there." He sees the nurse take out a rubber glove and put it on, snapping it to her hand. She lubes up the middle finger, smiles at him and tells him to roll over again.

"Now, this won't hurt a bit," she says, as she shoves her finger up his rear end. Pulling it in and out she leans over and says, "You like this, don't you?" He nods his head, looks up and sees the door open. In come three student doctors, all in gloves. They all take turns, poking and prodding his butt while he lays helpless and half-naked in his hospital bed, wearing only the top of the gown. How embarrassing. During all this he is hard as a rock, and finally comes right in the bed, in front of everyone. This happy patient can now take a nap!

Milk Anyone? There are a choice few that find breast milk an extreme turn on. We're not talking about men who have mates that are producing milk. These guys will go out of their way to find breast milk and it doesn't matter who it's from.

One particular gentleman asked that his fantasy take place in a bar. There would be dancing, a few drinks and a nice looking girl who'd ask to take him home for the night. *Sounds like what most guys want so far.* They get back to her place, get comfortable and begin to get busy. He notices that her breasts are hard and asks if they are real. She laughs and says that of course they are real. She takes his hand and places it on her breast, over her shirt. He begins to play when they start to leak, all over his hand. Surprised, he asks what is happening.

She tells him that she's breast-feeding and asks if he'd like to taste the milk. He agrees so she pulls down her shirt for him to try. He loves it and starts sucking harder, going from one breast to the other. He gets so turned on that he goes under her dress and tastes her everywhere. She rolls over on top of him and puts her breasts in his face. They have sex with her on top, dripping milk all over him. *At least he didn't ask to be diapered too.*

Choke On It, Baby: This call didn't start out to be unusual. A sociable, bubbly sounding man in his late thirties said he was a bit kinky. I asked him what was "kinky" to him. He said he wanted his fantasy to include a woman and two men. Agreed. Said he "liked to suck cock, liked it in the ass, and liked cum shots on his face." Nothing I haven't heard before. Not until he mentioned having a penis pushed down his throat until he choked did I agree that he was a bit kinky. Seems the choking is what was his turn on.

I gave him his fantasy with two men, one on the slender and average size who would be behind him and one bigger guy with everything big to match. He'd be the choker. The guy behind was gentler, while the guy in his mouth was rough. The woman would be instructing everyone and telling them what to do next. He enjoyed his fantasy, but especially being told, "Take it and choke on it, baby!" His voice would get louder and change octaves when he'd hear that, so he heard lots more like it! Must of liked it, he called back and I found numerous ways to gag and choke him.

Need A Clean Out? Can you guess by the title of this one that it's an enema fetish? It's not as uncommon as you might think and I do believe that this particular client really does use this fetish in a sexual way.

Apparently giving each other enemas turns on him and his girlfriend. Nothing and I mean nothing, grosses me out more than the thought of an enema or "poop" in general. So, with a shiver, I listened to him talk about how they do it in the bedroom and hold it as long as possible. Then they run to the bathroom for relief. They take turns, a couple of times each and when they're done, they have sex. *Well, at least they're clean if they like anal sex.*

Just telling me his story was turning him on. He asked me to hold on while he got his enema bag. When he returned, he described how he was pumping the water and asked if he could play with himself. I told him to enjoy, which he did. After some groans, he thanked me and said he'd be calling again, but for now, was going to the bathroom to relieve the pressure from holding all that water. All I can say is I'm glad I wasn't there.

Condom Man in Hosiery: This man's first fetish, which is wearing women's hosiery isn't all that different, but just wait. He also decided to visit a professional dominatrix and told me about his encounter. She had him come over and dressed him in lingerie, concentrating on the shoes and hosiery, which he seemed to enjoy best. The session included him ending up by masturbating over a paper towel on the floor for which he paid $150—$200, if I recall correctly. His next visit to her entailed going out in public to a shoe store wearing pantyhose under his slacks. She had him try on ladies shoes right there in front of the sales person, so that his stocking was showing. This turned him on. They also visited another place that caters to cross dressers. He paid more for this visit. Next time they went out he had to buy her a pair of boots on top of the fee.

He enjoys telling me about his sessions on the phone, but has always added a very odd request. He wants a used condom. Yup, that's right. Wants me to send him a used condom in the mail. Since I'm not going to grant his request, I tell him what I'd do if I were to send one. He'd have to call me before he opened it. I got creative and told him he'd need to microwave it for a few seconds to make it seem like it was fresh…*I know, that's a little nasty, but what the heck.* He'd be instructed to play with it and "squish" it in his fingers, then open it, slowly stick one finger in it and play with it. Lick his finger, lick the condom and then eat it. *Yeah, I know, that's really disgusting, but he likes it.*

He's was serious about the used condom and wondered how he could get one. Just too weird for me, but at any rate there's only one answer. A high price tag.

Please Pee On Me: I've included the now popular "golden shower" in this section. Although it's becoming more acceptable in sexual society, I still think it qualifies as "different," especially when taken to an extreme. I'm sure most would agree.

This phone client just loves women peeing on him. He also liked it combined with straight sex. He said he's had girlfriend's do it before but his fantasy is to have more than one girl. OK, we can accommodate that.

I told him he'd be brought into the bathroom and would enjoy a scented bath with lots of candles. In would come three ladies for him and while he sits in the tub, they all strip their clothing off as he enjoys look-ing at their beautiful nude bodies. He liked this already. One by one, they climb into the tub. *It's a really large tub.* They begin to kiss and touch him, everywhere. I described how the girls would reach under the water and play with him, rub their breasts on him, etc.

After he was totally turned on, the tub would be drained, leaving only an inch or two of water. He would lie back and the girls would line up, legs apart, standing over him and one by one, begin to pee on him. He would enjoy the "sweet warm yellow pee running all over his body from his neck to his legs." All he had to do was lie back and listen to it as it hit the water. As he stroked himself, they'd aim for his penis and he could come. He went nuts with this! I would hope he'd take a shower!

I'll Be Your Pee Boy: This guy said he wanted to be my slave and would do "anything" I demanded of him. He specifically wanted to be my pee boy and be my potty. Hmmm…what do I do with this fantasy?

I could tell that he was really into "slave" mode, so I told him if he was good and drew my bath water just right, lotioned and pedicured my feet, I might let him stay in the room with me when I sleep. He liked that. Asked if he should sleep on the floor. My response was that he'd have to sleep on the floor because my dogs sleep in the bed. *The dog part is actually true.* He wanted to be woken up during the night to be used as the potty. Being told he'd have to take every drop or else he'd be thrown out of the room turned him on. He liked being called names like, "nasty pee slave," "pee drinking potty boy," etc. and didn't talk too much, a lot of "Yes Mistress, No Mistress, Of course Mistress," was about it.

Told that he'd been a very good boy, his treat would be to watch one of the other Mistresses go poop and he could lick her butt. *Hey, I wasn't volunteering for that one, even in a fantasy!* He really delighted in this and the more pee he had to drink the better!

Same Guy—Different Story: On another call, he said he wanted to be really dirty and do nasty things. I asked him what he thought was nasty. He said "anything you can think of." Well, we won't get too crazy on him.

I told him he'd have to drink everyone's pee. All the Mistresses of the house. Before everyone went to bed, I'd have them file in one by one. All kinds of ladies. A blonde, redhead, brunette, black, etc. I would put a funnel in his mouth with a closing device on it. He'd have his hands tied behind his back and each girl would pee in the funnel. After one was finished, the clasp would be opened and the pee would pour down his throat. He wasn't allowed to gag or spit it out. He had to drink it all. He was enjoying this, so I went on to describe that each girl would pee more than the previous one. He'd keep saying he would take "every drop" and "not miss anything." "I'm your toilet," was his favorite saying. That's a good slave. And so it goes with the pee drinking potty boy.

A Very Creepy Situation: A man called and said he had a really different fantasy. Well, nothing weird about the sex, just regular sex. OK I thought, what could be weird about that? It was where he wanted to have sex. In a casket. Yeah, a casket. I wanted to make sure he fantasized about having sex with a live woman in this casket. Thankfully he did. I told him I had keys to my uncle's funeral parlor since I do the entire flower arranging in the place. *For the record, that isn't true, just in case you're wondering although once I took a friend on a tour of a funeral home because he was curious. The funeral director was a friend.*

I tell him he has to be quiet as we creep into the place with just a flashlight. We go into the room that has the caskets for people to buy. He picks a shiny black one with white satin on the inside. As he undresses, I put flowers by the coffin and light candles. He wants his girl, me in this case, to undress and put the clothing in the casket next to us. I described how it would feel to climb in to the coffin, putting his hands on the cool outside of it while slipping naked onto the soft satin. When he was in, he could look around and see the candles flickering and smell the flowers. Not bad, considering most people inside those things can't smell or see!

He's getting more and more turned on with all the descriptions so I figured I'd better get to the sex. I kept saying that "your girl" would climb in with you because I just couldn't bring myself to say, "I would climb in with you." Just too creepy. Anyhow, I told him that he and his girl would enjoy passionate sex with her on top. He'd see her hair lit up by the candles and she'd continue to ride him until they were both satisfied. Then she'd take a flower and place it in the coffin while they both relaxed for a while. *Nice touch, huh?*

Poopie Man: Yeah, you know there had to be one of those in here didn't you? If you ever wondered whether or not poop fetishes were real, I'm telling you, they are. We know there are some people who smear chocolate all over their faces, take pictures and put them on the internet for amusement, but these are serious poopie people. It turns them on. *Where are they when I have to clean my backyard every week due to three big dogs?*

Anyway, this one client not only likes poop but also likes to be made fun of, called names and humiliated. I suggest that if you're eating something, you put it down for the next part. I told him he was bad and needed to strip naked and crawl on his hands and knees on a cold floor. Then he'd be dragged by a rope around his neck to the bathroom, stare at the floor and be called names. How he's "good for nothing," a "nasty dirty slut," and a "worthless piece of shit." He's only worth a pile of shit and I'm going to prove it to him, but first he has to be peed on. A male slave can come in and pee on him. Then, maybe he should be pooped on. No, he's not worth being pooped on. A nasty slave can poop on the floor while he watches. Then I'll hold his head over the poop and call him more names until I shove his face in it. He must eat it all. This drives the guy wild! *The only benefit about this story is that I don't feel like eating for some time, so it's a great on those "fat days."*

Same Guy—Different Poop Story: He called another time, saying he was worthless and needed to be pooped on. I told him that as before, he wasn't worth it, but I knew what he should do. He'd have to crawl again to the bathroom on all fours while having his rear spanked with a wet ruler. Then he was to wait by the toilet until a slave pooped. His hands would be tied behind him and he'd have his face pushed into the toilet. The object would be to pick up each turd with his teeth and place them one by one on the floor. (Ewwww…!) After he did that, he must eat them all with his hands still tied. *He really lapped that one up!*

A Funny Poop Story: This isn't anywhere near as gross as the above stories. It's really amusing even though anyone reading this will think I'm a complete nut case. A man with a poop fetish said that what really turns him on is to watch a girl go to the bathroom, or in this case, listen. He asked if I had to go. No, I didn't. I tried just talking about "bathroom stuff," but he kept interrupting and asking if I was sure I didn't have to go. He kept asking me to "please try." Hmmmm….think.

Well, I could at least flush the toilet for him and pretend I did try. On my way to the bathroom, I went by a bowl of fruit on the table and had a weird thought. I grabbed a couple of grapes and told him I'd try my hardest to poop. He wanted to hear the noises one makes when trying to go. Really peculiar, I know. I must have had a glass or two of wine that day; cause here's what I did. I put the phone near the toilet and dropped a grape into the bowl while pretending to poop. You know those mini poops? Yes, I really did this. He was thrilled so I did it again, two more times. When I put the phone back to my ear he gave a wonderful sigh and said "Thank you…that was great!" *I really am nutty!*

Diaper Poop: Just one more poop story. This one is really bizarre. A guy called and said he liked to be treated as an adult baby, diapered and such in front of others. OK, I've talked about this stuff before. I told him he'd be made to wear a diaper in front of all my lady friends and have to suck on a pacifier, drink from a baby bottle and speak baby talk. He'd have to crawl instead of walk and cry when his diaper was wet, although he wasn't supposed to wet his diaper as he was potty training.

Then he went on to say he liked to be tied up. When I started to talk about taking belts and tying up his hands and feet, he sounded really excited. He wanted to know if the ladies were going to leave him there for a while. I told him that they would leave him for a long time. He asked what to do if he had to go to the bathroom and I said he had to "hold it." He said he pooped in his diaper. I told him he was a bad boy and needed to be punished.

Now, at this point, I have no idea what kind of punishment he'd like in his fantasy so I suggested a spanking. Apparently that wasn't good enough. He mentioned that the last "baby-sitter" made him eat the poop while he was tied up. *Not my idea of the girl next door.* So, his penalty would be his diaper taken off and put over his face. Then it would be smeared in and he had to lick his lips clean. Yuck! He called a few more times and the nastier the better.

The Roman Emperor (Oooo...He's a Mean One): This guy has a couple of fantasies. First of all he likes to dress up when we're talking. Cross dress I mean. He likes to dress "slutty" and wear stockings, heels and a trashy outfit, completing it with makeup and a wig. He'll say he wants to be a slave, clean the house be spanked and told what to do, even humiliated. I'll ask him if he's a little slut, a naughty sissy boy and bad for wearing his wife's underwear. He'll say he is all of the above, especially since she doesn't know he has them and gets them stained. Then he puts them back in her drawer. That's not very nice, now is it?

Just as I'm thinking that his fantasies are not so out there, he goes on the say that he'd like to be slave to a mean Roman Emperor. *Where did this come from?* OK, I guess we can invite him along. Then he tells me if the Emperor finds out he's really a boy, he'll get mad and cut off his testicles. OUCH! He says the emperor likes to make bad boys into eunuchs.

Now in the very old days, when these things did happen, the poor guys had no say in the matter, but for someone to seriously fantasize and want this is news to me. He likes to hear that if he's caught he'll be turned into a eunuch. This man is extremely polite and doesn't sound like he's too aroused, but I guess he is. All of a sudden he'll get really turned on and end the call. Sometimes with a polite "Goodbye," or with really loud moans and groans.

Roman 11: In one of his fantasies, he's dressed as a eunuch and is slave to a Queen. He looks androgynous, is wearing makeup, has long hair and wears jewelry. He's busy getting the Queens clothing ready while other slaves bathe her. He brushes her long beautiful hair after her bath while the others tend to her lotion. When finished, the slaves line up for the Emperor to come in and inspect. It's the mean one again.

He comes in with all his guards stopping at the door, looks at the slaves and goes down the line checking them to see if they're aroused. They have all been castrated so they can't get an erection. This way, they can't have sex and are no threat to anyone. When he gets to our phone guy, he notices that he has an erection and orders him to strip. He does as told and is ordered to be castrated. The Emperor has him turned into a eunuch and he's made to dress like a girl from then on.

He doesn't always invite the Emperor along. Sometimes it's just "us girls."

Bite Me! Yup, biting fetishes. We're not talking about a little love bite here or a nibble. No. Real biting, to leave marks and bruises.

This started out as a "normal" sex call, with talk of getting naked and lots of kissing. Then he said "I want you to bite me on the ear." OK I thought. I'll tell him he'd get his ear nibbled. No, that wasn't good. He wanted to be bitten. So, I said I'd bite his earlobe, hard. He remarked with an, "Oh that hurts, but I love it. Bite me more!" I told him I was going down his neck and to his nipples. Then they'd get bitten. "Oh look, I left tooth marks." That made him crazy, so I continued. "I'm going down to your stomach now with my tongue, down your legs and to your inner thigh. Now I'm going to bite your inner thigh because it's so sensitive there." He loved it.

I wasn't sure if I should go as far as his toes so I stayed around the body area, telling him I was going to lick his hard cock now. I wasn't sure what the heck he'd want until he said, "Bite it!" I don't have a penis, but I could feel the pain! I told him I'd bite the head, then up and down until he got as hard as possible. When he got really hard I told him to stroke it while I bit his balls. That did it. He didn't even make it to a ten-minute call!

Think of what this guy would look like if he really did this stuff, and who knows, maybe he does. I'd hate to be the girlfriend who he's mad at for something. One look at him and any judge would slap a restraining order on the girl and she'd have to go to abuse classes!

Scratch Me!: Similar to the "bite me" story, but with nails. This guy said he had a fetish for long nails and wanted to know how long mine were. He said he liked nails that were three inches. Wow, that's long. I said mine were about that long. *OK, so I lied.*

I asked if he'd like the nails moved up and down his back and chest. He said yes, but do it hard. I told him to lie on his stomach and I'd give him a nail massage, running them all over. Here I am on the phone asking him, "Do you feel that? Tell me how it is." His response was "Mmmmm….that's nice but do it harder." "OK, I'm scratching your back now. Can you feel it?" "Oh yes, that's great." I tell him that I'm leaving red marks on his back. "Oh yes, that's what I want!" Good….now I know I've got him going and found his hot spots.

I tell him to turn over and I'll take care of his chest. Then I ask if he wants some great sex. "Oh yes, now!" I tell him I'm going to jump on that big hard cock and scratch his chest while we have sex. He's ecstatic now, especially when I describe the marks on his chest from the nails. "I'm going down your arms now. I can't help going faster and harder with the nails. Oh no! I've made you bleed!" His voice was shaking by this time. I told him I'd finish by scratching his face so hard that everyone would know he belonged to me. *Or had a fight with a bobcat!* He only called a couple of times. Maybe he bought a big cat after all!

I Want To Watch You In The Potty: I'm sure you've heard of plenty of video cameras that film people in their everyday life to be broadcast on the internet. Nothing too new, but nevertheless, I think that getting aroused by watching someone take a dump should be in the "odd fetish" section. The shower, I can certainly understand but poop watching? Quite another story.

This guy spoke of putting a video camera in his house so he could watch his wife and her friends going "number two." *I hope he's kidding and didn't really do that.* I wasn't sure what to say to him so I asked questions, like, "Tell me what you saw. What happened with your wife? Tell me about her friends. Were they all thin? Any fat bums on the pot?" Just stupid questions. He went into describing the different poops they made.

Grossed me out, I have to say. I'm hardened to a lot of this stuff, but that is a definite story you want to hear before you're thinking about a food binge. Spoils the appetite for sure!

I asked him what he'd do with the video. He said he was going to make still photos of each girl's dirty bum in the toilet and put the photos on the wall. *OK….this guy needs help*. Thankfully, he never called again.

Wierdos

As I said in the very beginning, there have been a few. The ones that I'd classify as "weirdoes" aren't just guys acting stupid or playing games. I honestly think they're messed up in the head. These guys don't even classify in the section for odd fetishes. These are people that can do harm to others. I'd love to get the handwriting of these guys to analyze! One was either playing a mean joke or he was just a whacko. He was paid back accordingly, as you'll see. Here are a few notables:

First, there are those who requested weird things that I will not accommodate even on a phone call: Among them are:

*Sex with animals.
*Sex with the dead, people that is.
*Sex with kids. I DON'T THINK SO BUDDY!
*Sex with mom, dad, or other incestuous relationships.
There are TV shows for that!
*Rape fantasies.
*Blood fantasies—cutting people and ingesting their blood.

Some specific people:

I'm A Prisoner!: Very new to the sex line, a guy called from my area and wanted a domination call. He told me that he had a mistress who kept him prisoner in his house, would tie him up overnight and up to twenty-four hours. Said her aunt would come in also, beat him and force him to have sex with her (the aunt, that is). He combined this with adult baby fetishes and said he'd be diapered and left tied for days only allowed up to eat. He sounded SO upset and I believed him for some reason.

He called a few times and on the fourth call, said his Mistress wanted him to be castrated. He wanted to know if he should do it. Ordinarily, I'd go along with fantasies, like the Emperor and the Eunuch, but this guy sounded nuttier than a fruitcake. I told him not to do it. He'd keep calling and saying how he must do it and it must be done while I'm listening. I told him I'd help by giving the police his number and they could come and arrest the Mistress and her Aunt. He never called again!

The Payphone Nut Case: This guy bugged me off and on for over two years. I had just begun the phone line when a soft-spoken man called, asked the regular questions and gave me a credit card. I processed it and it came up "invalid," which means that the card number is wrong. He gave me the info again with the same results. He said he'd get a different card and call back. I like to have a base phone number to call clients back, but he explained that he couldn't receive incoming calls. *Remember that I'm still very new at this point.* He gave another card number. Same thing.

In between calls, I checked and found that "invalid" usually means a bogus number. I'm getting annoyed with him now. Out of fake cards I guess, he asked if I liked leather coats, saying he'd send one if I'd do a call with him. I was new, but not stupid! If this happened now, I'd simply hang up and not deal with him. I pay for the 800 number he called on and wouldn't let him waste my time or money. My policy now is that if one doesn't have a phone number I can call them back on, one doesn't get a call. I finally hung up.

He called a couple more times that day and I told him I wouldn't talk to him. He tried again the next day. His voice was recognizable even though he'd change his name. After the same lines of crap and recognizing the same payphone numbers he'd call from, I'd tell him I didn't want to talk to him, ever. Then I'd hang up. He'd call back, over and over again until I'd answer. Sometimes twenty or thirty times in a row, which would tie up my phone line as well as aggravate me. If I was out and had calls forwarded, the answering machine would pick which again would cost me money every time this idiot got through.

I finally got SO annoyed that I yelled at him. Something like, "Don't you EVER call me again, you f***ing idiot!" Guess what? HE CALLED AGAIN ! He was the most persistent man I'd ever encountered. I can't believe he had nothing else better to do. So, I'd pick up the phone and get even nastier to him, blowing whistles in his ear, yelling and cursing him, calling him names and even telling him I knew where he was and that I called the cops. Nothing worked. He just kept calling.

A male friend suggested that maybe he LIKED being talked to this way and that he's getting his jollies, free. Good point. So the next time he called I asked him if he knew he was a "piece of shit who wasn't worth the toilet paper to wipe on." He said yes! My friend was right. Next time he called, I quietly asked him what he wanted and why he kept calling me. He said he wanted to "date" me. *Sure buddy, in a heartbeat.* Well, I told him he'd have to write something to me and drop it off at the office of the magazine I advertised with in his area to have his handwriting analyzed. He of course said he would, but didn't.

When he called back, I told him simply that I was disappointed that he didn't follow directions, was going to hang up now and never speak to him again. I hung up. He called back. I hung up. On and on with this now. I'd take the phone off the hook. He'd give up for the evening and try the next night. I figured if I was consistent, like punishing a kid and meaning what you say, he'd stop. He did for a while.

He'd get smart and call from different numbers in other towns that I didn't know. A couple of times he fooled me and I'd begin to answer a few questions. Then I'd just say: "You know what? Uh…NO." and hang up. He hasn't called in a while and when he does and asks for Marie I just hang up. No words, nothing. Mr. payphone man, get a damn life! And if you're ever anywhere near me, I hope you know what a 209A is!

Rubber Doll Man: This one is a scream. I hope this guy doesn't date 'cause when she finds out the way he treats his rubber dolly, she'll be out of there.

Now I'm not insulting anyone who owns a rubber doll. I'm sure they have their place, but it's the way this guy talked to the doll that made me nervous. *Yes, he talked to her.* He said he was an older man in his early sixties and spoke in a very soft, musical voice. It started off to be a regular sex type call. He told me he had a nice hard on and was horny a lot. Kept talking about panties and smelling the ass of the underwear. *OK, whatever.* THEN he said he had a rubber "dolly" there with him. I could actually hear him caressing what sounded to me like rubber.

He said he loved to play with her and wanted to stick his cock in her mouth. Then he'd say things like, "You want me to do that to you, right?" I'd avoid the question as I felt something wasn't right with this guy. Then he said how he'd stick it in every hole he could find and how he thought I'd like the same thing. I tried talking calmly to him and after a half-hour, he ended the first call.

He called again, asking for photos. I had an advertisement that said "free photo" with call. Figured that at the very least I'd have his name and address, so I sent a couple. He called when he received them and said he was disappointed that they weren't nudes. I'd already told him I don't take nudes. He was upset. I ended the call with an excuse of some sort.

When he called the last time, he was back to the rubber doll. This time he said he was going to be rough with her and rape her. "I'm going to get on top of her and rape her!" he said. I told him he could do whatever he wants to the doll, but not to ever use that word again. That was the last call, thankfully. So, rubber doll man......if you're reading this, DON'T call me, ever again. Call a therapist instead.

The Tennis Ball Guy: This one will either make you laugh your butt off or throw up. Either way, it's interesting, true and really strange.

A younger man called and talked about things like oral sex, regular sex, girlfriends, etc. I didn't think much of it. Then he mentioned anal sex and how he liked it. OK, still not strange. II figured he had his girlfriend use dildo's on him and wanted to talk about that as well.

He said he likes his girlfriend to put three fingers up his ass, then four, five and finally her whole fist. Should I believe this? I let him continue. He wanted me to tell him how I'd stick my fist up his rear and make the "sounds" as I punched it in him harder and harder. He wanted "sounds" and for me to say things like, "You like that, don't you?"….(push sound) and "How does that feel?" (more pushing sounds).

Then he went to the feet. Said his girlfriend stuck her big toe up his butt and then her whole foot. She must have a size four shoe! He then said he was going to stick tennis balls up his ass while I talked to him. He wanted me to tell him how I was kicking my foot in his butt while making the pushing noises and tell him to stick another ball up his ass. He'd say he had three up there and then would play with himself. Come on now, are you serious? This is just a wee bit crazy!

The last time he called, he had a girl with him, who sounded drunk or high. At first she came to the phone to say hello, I mean, slur hello. This girl claimed she was 22 and was going to suck him and stick tennis balls up his ass. They were laughing and carrying on in the background while I was on speakerphone. They both sounded so messed up that I couldn't handle either one of them anymore. I told her to get the hell out of there, find a better guy and find better ways to spend her spare time. I told him he was far too much for me and that he's gonna have an ongoing case of the shits if he keeps sticking tennis balls up his ass. The end of that guy.

The FREAK: Believe me, you'll agree with calling this guy a freak. He's earned the title. A man calls with a nice soft voice, gives his description to me and at first sounded OK. I asked him what he'd like me to do for him.

He said, domination, being the submissive one. I told him that domination could be anything from being my little boy-toy sex slave, to spanking, humiliation, cross dressing, dildos, on and on and to be a bit more specific. He said he liked to be hit physically. I think I told him I was going to tie him naked to a chair and with a cat tail whip, start at his feet and go up, giving special attention to his "huge" cock as he put it. He wanted me to hit him harder with the whip. I told him I was going to give it to him real good.

Here's where it gets freaky. He said he wanted me to hit him with a baseball bat. Huh? A what?" I asked. He repeated, a baseball bat. As I'm trying to digest this strange request he "hits" me with another crazy request, no pun intended. He wanted the bat wrapped in barbed wire. I'm thinking that he's just kidding but he wasn't. He sounded "dead" serious. *I just can't help it with the puns.*

Now I'm getting a little upset with this guy. I said something like, "My dear, what you're asking isn't domination. It's assault and battery with a deadly weapon!" He talked about fighting in some sort of "death matches" where they use barbed wired bats. Now I think he's obviously fantasizing, but it's still freaky. Oh…it gets much worse.

I told him I wouldn't take part in such violent fantasies and preferred to end the call. He turned the tables on me and said that he was going to "cut of my tits and stuff them down my throat." I'd probably be left to bleed to death. Excuse me? That pissed me off, big time! I won't put into quotes exactly what I said to him because I'd get locked up, but I did tell the jerk I have a very feisty Italian temper, which he should leave alone. He kept laughing and saying he was a clown. You're a f***ing clown allright! I told him off again. He called himself some "clown names" I'd never heard of, laughed and hung up. I was SO mad I think I could have hit the freak with the damn bat!

*Note: I don't want to be specific about what he said because I have nothing against the people that I later found out he was trying to imitate. He was doing these entertainers a grave injustice.

What did I do with that fiery Italian temper that was riled up? Made a phone call. No, not that! I called the FBI and gave them his name and information. Hey, if he were some sort of killer, they'd be able to check him out. If he was just a nut without a record, he might think twice next time.

Then I got the idea to call a friend that for some strange reason I thought would be able to shed light on this weird ass freak. He did. Apparently the nut had me all freaked out for nothing. *Oops….already called the authorities.* My friend actually repeated word for word what the weirdo said to me. Now I really got worried! He was apparently reciting song lyrics, believe it or not, and obviously knew I had no clue. I got him back though. The particular band he was quoting has a huge following of very serious fans that don't appreciate people like him. So, his number was given out to plenty of them. I'm sure they called and gave him hell for it. He deserved everything he got and will think twice before he threatens someone's life again.

I Only Come Out At Night: This guy said he was really a vampire. OK, I'll go with the fantasy. Many people are intrigued by vampires, clothing, etc. We talked about dressing up, lighting candles and only playing at night. He told me he had fangs permanently put onto his top canine teeth. I've seen this before, no big deal. He talked about taking a beautiful naked girl under his large cape would make love to her and turn her into a vampire. *Some would consider this a bit romantic.*

Now he spoils it by saying he wants to bite someone, specifically me, on the breast and suck my blood. *OK, now we're getting into weird territory.* He says he's gonna bite the other one and then do the same on my inner thighs. He wanted to drink it and write things on the wall in the blood. Again, I got irritated.

I quietly asked him if he was really a vampire. He said he absolutely was a real one. I changed my tone of voice and said: "Well then you'd know that all that mumbo jumbo about mirrors, the dark, crosses and stakes is a bunch of made up bullshit. So, I don't believe you. I think you're just nuts." I think I put a "fucking" before the "nuts" and said it would be a contest to see who'd get who's blood first if he ever really said that stuff to me. I said a few more choice things, told him he should get in his damn coffin, shut the lid and never open it again and abruptly hung up. I guess I just don't take kindly to people telling me how they're going to cut me up.

*Note: No offense to anyone who's interested in vampires, clothing, music, etc. I personally own some music that is considered to be "vampire." I'm also familiar with certain bloodletting practices that are supposed to be done carefully. Everybody has his or her own tastes. *Oops, did it again.* BUT, biting someone over and over, drinking his or her blood and smearing it on the wall is just TOO MUCH.

Powder Puff Man: Another domination type caller. Wanted to be hypnotized with a powder puff. Huh? Try me again on that? He claimed to have visited a Mistress who hypnotized him by blowing powder at him with her puff. *This time I mean face powder.* I generally speak to the client on a "normal" level, and then we get into the role-play. This guy NEVER got out of character, from the first time he called. He'd ask me if I was swinging a diamond necklace back and forth while I spoke to him because he felt like he was under a spell. Even asked me how he could break the spell from the other Mistress.

He eventually got on my nerves with this so I told him to break the spell by not calling and his wife would never see the credit card bills, therefore avoiding a possible hypnotic "hit up the side of the head."

Cross Dress Me

Why do men call me to talk about cross-dressing? Many reasons. Some I can explain some I can't. Here's what I think. In the times we live in, women are allowed to express all of their sides. We can wear a beautiful gown one day and the next clothed in jeans, sneakers and a baseball hat. We even wear combat boots and camouflage clothing. Put a guy in a pink miniskirt with pumps and make up and see how many strange looks he gets! Men are criticized for expressing their feminine side. Sure, they can be well groomed, wear cologne and gel their hair, but can they use blush if they look pale and get away with it? Not really. Think about it ladies. When we're all dressed up we are treated differently than when we're in those army boots. Doors are opened and we're protected as the "delicate flowers that we are." Maybe the men need to feel like that sometimes not always being the "big, strong guy."

We've already encountered men who wear ladies lingerie. Others like to cross dress completely, including makeup, wigs and padding. There are those who keep it at home and some who take it out, or would like to. Some men talk about having sex with a woman while cross-dressed, some want a dildo and still others want another man involved. This section could go on forever, but I'll try to keep it down.

Let's Put On Our Nighties and Play: Probably the mildest of the cross dressers would go to a man about sixty who simply likes to wear lingerie. He'll call me and describe his outfit. It's usually a black or red lace teddy including thigh high stockings and sheer bikini underwear. He'll say he's wearing lipstick and I always remind him to dab on some nice perfume for a more feminine effect.

This particular gentleman has absolutely no feminine tone in his voice when he asks me what I'd be wearing if I were with him. I'll tell him I'd love to wear a pretty white lace corset for him with a g-string and white lace stockings, along with pretty silver heels, curled hair and sparkling makeup. He'll say he's getting so hard and that his cock is bulging out of the panties. If I were there he'd rub it against my rear end to show me how hard he is. Then I'd turn around, stroke him and still in our lingerie, have sex while looking in the mirror. Mild…very, very mild.

Transform Me into a She-Male: This one is complicated. The gentle-man is very specific about what he wants. His calls last a half-hour or more and I have to do ALL the talking. He gives almost no input. Just listens. There have been many variations to his story. Here are some samples.

He wants to be "tricked" as a male into staying with a beautiful Oriental woman who he's totally attracted to and would do anything for. She tells him he can stay if he works for her, serving at a party she's having for all her girlfriends. Fine with him. One catch. He has to dress like a woman, a feminine little maid. He does it, but needs improvement. He can work again if he tries harder. Agreed. She trains him, teaches him how to use makeup, walk like a girl, and makes him shave his legs and wear false nails. He does better the next few times and she lets him stay with her. Over a period of time, his hair grows long, his nails grow and he's slowly transforming into a she-male.

The beautiful woman gives him "vitamin drinks" which are filled with hormones. He loses facial hair and his hips and rear fill out. So do his breasts. Now she's got him in her power and he must become her sex slave. She calls him a slut and pimps him out to clients as a prostitute. He must fool them into thinking he's really a girl and must always keep his penis hidden. She teaches him to suck a dildo and then gives him the real thing. If he doesn't do a good enough job, she denies him his special drink and denies him even the sight of her. He is so addicted to her he'll do anything. He takes care of all her male clients, giving them the best blowjobs ever. She still doesn't think he's feminine enough, so she buys him breast implants, gives him a tattoo and pierces his body with pretty jewelry.

*Note: During the early conversations he'd ask questions, a lot of them, such as, "What am I wearing? What does my hair look like? How long are my nails and how are they painted? Do I have any piercings or tattoos? How does my make up look? Describe it. Do I have any jewelry on? What does the woman look like? What is HER makeup like? What is SHE wearing? What does HER hair look like?" On and on like that, which is why I say I have to talk the entire time. Making up all those details isn't that easy.

Back to the story. The woman is now satisfied with the way he looks but still calls him names because he's a "virgin." He tells her he doesn't want to be one anymore but she makes him wait and wait, continuing to be her sex slave. After a long time, she decides it's time for him to become a "real woman." She sets up a special time and special outfits, which I have to describe in detail, and instructs him on what to do.

She stands in front of him and slowly strips, letting him feel her beautiful breasts and pretty rear end. She faces away from him and removes her little panties and when she turns around, she has a BIG COCK of her own. He's shocked but pleased at the same time. He is told to suck it, which he does very well. Then she teases his "boy pussy" with her big cock until she has sex with him. He must beg for it. He then says "thank you" and tells me to have a nice day. No real chit chat. Just ends the call. I really use my imagination on this caller, trying to describe things differently every time he calls so he won't be bored. It's a challenge, believe me!

*Note: It's too detailed to remember, so I cheat. I keep a ladies magazine next to me and pre-pick a couple of photos. I describe the hair, makeup and clothing. So much easier!

Split Personality: This man calls from the same number, pretending to be two different people. One likes women, is more aggressive and likes to watch. The other is more soft spoken, submissive and has a man involved. This is all okay, but I have to admit I've gotten really upset with him for some of his silly calls. Example: He'd called to see if anyone else was around to do a three-way call, preferably a man. I told him that the man who helps me with these calls works until 5:00 PM, every day, period. He hangs up and five minutes later calls and says he's the other guy! When I ask him what he'd like, he says the same damn thing! Does he really think I'm that stupid or does he really believe he's two separate people? Strange.

When he's person #1: Let's call him Tim. He's very submissive, speaks softly, and tries to sound feminine. I ask him what he's dressed in and the usual response is panties, hose and a bra. I tell him he looks so pretty and girlish but since he's in such revealing underwear, he looks slutty. I instruct him to walk around the room, look at himself in the mirror and strike a few poses to show me how much like a girl he can be. At this point, a woman with very large breasts comes in and wants to have a threesome. I have him parade around the room for her and tell her to call him a little slut. He loves it and asks what we're going to do with him. We tell him to watch at first while she and I get into it. Soon after, we turn our attention to him, making him please us both before we get out a big strap on and give it to him good.

Person #2: We'll call him Ron. He has a much stronger manly tone about him and is more outgoing. His favorite call goes like this: I phone my male friend, for real, and call Ron to make it a three-way call. Everyone says hi. My friend, "Mick," is a straight man in his fifties but is a natural on the phone. Sometimes I don't say much at all.

I tell Ron that he'll walk in while I'm getting it on with Mick. Of course we ask Ron to come in and watch for a while. I tell Mick that Ron seems lonely and invite him to participate. He comes over and we both undress him. I push Ron's face down to suck my friend. This makes Mick very happy and he decides to have sex with Ron. I tell Ron to bend over and take all nine inches at once. *Now my friend comes in hot and heavy.* Mick tells Ron he's going to give him all he's got, hard and fast. He gets very descriptive and asks Ron how he likes getting pounded by a big hard cock. We can hear Ron's breathing heavy.

As with all of his calls, they don't last too long and he hangs up abruptly about ninety percent of the time. On occasion, he says "thanks" and hangs up just as fast.

Cross dress and Embarrass Me: One guy who was pretty young, 24 or so, asked to be cross-dressed forcibly and publicly. Hmmm. How do I do that one? I know. I told him we were in the city on the third floor of a building. The big front window was open and we could see the people and cars on the street below. I would put him in front of the window and make him strip naked. People would start to notice a naked man on the third floor just standing in the window. When they'd stop to stare, I'd start dressing him.

I'd make him sit facing me and hand him white lace stockings to wear. Then he'd stand up and face the window again, stepping into some pink and white lace panties. Add to that a matching bra and a white lace garter belt. I'd hook the two back garters and then tell him to turn around with his butt to the window while I fastened the other two. How embarrassing for him. He'd be made up in lipstick and eyeshadow and told to dance around in the window area. Now the people have gathered downstairs to watch and there is a crowd.

When there are enough people, he must masturbate in front of everyone through the panties, not removing them or exposing himself. Of course, everyone watching knows he's a man, by his build as well as his nice hard on. When he comes in front of the crowd he can be free to take the girl clothing off and leave. He liked this fantasy. I just hope he never really tries it and gets arrested for lude behavior!

Call the Personal's: This man called often and talked about masturbating in front of someone. This time he called to say he'd responded to a personal ad in the paper. Said it was another man in the ad. I had NO idea he had bi tendencies. They met for the first time at a large department store where they shopped together for lingerie. Afterward they went home and dressed for each other.

My phone client, let's call him Jon, said it was his first experience with a man and he loved it. The man in the personal ad was considerably older than Jon; in his sixties I believe and enjoyed dressing up just as much. Jon told me that he gave his first "blow job," enjoyed the taste and "having a man in his mouth" very much. He said that he had sex six times! Twice orally, twice in the butt, also his first time and twice Jon masturbated for him. *Six? Is that possible?* Wonder if Jon will be completely gay now or if he'll still like women. Time will tell.

Some Panty Confessions I've heard:

Guys call and tell me things they wouldn't ordinarily admit to. Some of the confessions are about their panty adventures. Here are some of them.

*They've taken their wife's panties to wear and the wife wonders where in the heck they are.

*They take their wife's undies and she knows it, but when asked, the reply is, "Huh? Nope I don't have em."

*They've bought panties for themselves and said it was for a girlfriend.

*Bought panties and actually let the salesperson know exactly who they were for.

*Wore panties to work, often.

*Wore pantyhose to work, under dress pants and mens dress socks.

*Masturbating with underwear wrapped around their penis.

Some bi sex/gay confessions

*One guy called for a male massage and ended up with a hand job.

*One guy called for a male massage and ended up giving his first blowjob.

*One guy called a male escort and ended up having anal sex for the first time, both giving and receiving.

*A guy called a personal ad and started up a sexual relationship with another man.

Bad Girls

How can I leave out those men who like to dominate, give spankings and be the "big daddy?" Honestly, there are so many more callers who would rather be dominated than dominate. Why? Maybe because they can really act out a fantasy/role play with their ladies involving a spanking but not to the extent they do it on the phone. *Sometimes, they go a little crazy.* You'll see why.

*Note: To repeat myself, any caller asking to be the "daddy" or the "teacher" goes by my rules. He has to be the "step-dad" or the "professor" with an adult student. I know that with some phone lines, absolutely anything goes, but I don't want to encourage anyone who might really have incest fantasy or want sex with a teen or preteen kid. I've only had a few callers who wouldn't agree. They went elsewhere I'm sure.

The Professor: This man called with the "teacher/schoolgirl" scenario. I said it would have to be a "professor/college student," which was fine with him. He just wanted the idea of the submissive student.

Now, our "teacher" had his own set of rules. The outfit worn by the schoolgirl had to be precise. Pleated skirt, white cotton blouse, knee socks with flat shoes, a white cotton bra and panties. The panties could be bikini briefs but no thong or g-string and the bra had to be full coverage. Teacher got very upset if the student didn't have the proper underwear on.

The girl is called to his room because she's not doing well in his class. He offers her an "A" if she does what he says. If she doesn't get an A, her parents won't pay for next semester. What a spot she's in. *I get to play the part of the college girl. What a stretch that is! I'm not shy, young OR submissive!* She shyly complies. Our professor isn't a sweet man. He's very demanding and likes to treat his student rough. He tells her to pull up her skirt so that he can see her underwear. He bends her over the desk and pats her bottom. Then he spanks her with a ruler because she's not paying attention in class. He tells her to keep her underwear around her ankles now while he goes to the other side of the desk and exposes his big penis. She has to suck it for as long as he says. He tells her how she has to come every day and do this or she won't get an "A."

She must answer "Yes Sir" when she's allowed to speak. He goes behind her and gives her his nine inches hard and fast, pulling her ponytail while he pumps. He tells her he's going to pump her in the ass now, also hard and fast. When he's had enough, he goes around to her face and strokes himself until he comes. It's all over her face and hair. She can wash her face but must leave her hair all sticky, all day, to remind her who the boss is.

He's actually asked me for pictures in the schoolgirl outfit but I think I'm just a "wee bit" too mature for that kind of dress up. There's plenty of ladies wearing schoolgirl outfits for him to view.

More Bad Behavior:

Some guys will ask questions and when they get the answers they want, decide on the punishment. Such as:

*Have you been a bad girl, wearing that short skirt today?

*All my guy friends saw your panties when you bent over. I know you did it on purpose.

*I saw you flirting with my brother! (Uncle, cousin, etc.)

*I know you kissed my brother! (Uncle, cousin, etc.)

*I know you had sex with my brother! (Uncle, cousin, etc.)

The punishment is usually a good spanking from a bare hand to a ruler. Most guys like the bare hand on the bare butt. There's almost always sex involved.

Yes Mistress—No Mistress:

These are the domination calls. I've touched on some, as many of the fetish calls include domination. These are the calls for the serious minded guy who wants to be told what to do. Some are on the mild side, the client wanting to be a house or sex slave, while the broader range includes restraints, spankings, whippings, shocks and more. They all must use terms such as, "Mistress," or "Maam" when they speak and don't really make any requests, because they're not allowed to. So how do I know what they want? Some will tell me before we begin and I run with it. Some don't say much so I'll ask questions during their phone fantasy. The way to handle this is to find out what they're into the first time they call and go from there. Warning: Some get a little freaky, but you should be used to it by now.

Suspend and Restrain Me: "Make me as uncomfortable as possible," is my translation of these calls. This is a quiet, shy sounding guy in his thirties who lives at home with his mom, is unmarried and has some serious fetishes. Here's how a couple of our calls have gone.

Restrain Me: I ask if he has prepared himself for me. He tells me he's naked with his cock and balls tied in addition to an uncomfortable "cock ring." Now, even though I don't have a penis, I can imagine how it would feel to put a soft one through metal rings and then get turned on. Ouch! Has to hurt!....Anyway, I tell him he's a good boy, but to be sure he remembers to be a loyal slave, he must smack himself ten times on both his penis and balls. *I'm easy on him.* I think he really does smack himself but the rest is a total fantasy. He wants to know what I'd do to him next.

He's told he'd be tied to a chair in a dark room with a light on him. Nipple clamps would be added to further the discomfort. A "slave girl" would be brought in, naked, on her hands and knees and led over to him. She'd have to twist and pinch the clamps, which would add pain and make him hard. *Sure...this makes sense.* She'd be tall and slender with jet-black hair and chocolate colored skin. (His choice) His chair would be leaned all the way back and she'd be pushed down on his face, nearly smothering him with her hairy pussy. He'd have to lick her until she'd come in his mouth, taking all her juices and holding them without swallowing. Now it would be her turn. She's forced down on his penis, still tied and bound, and must suck him until he comes in her mouth. She must also hold it without swallowing. *This whole thing was his idea.*

He's put upright and she's pushed on top of his cock. His hands are now tied behind her back and the same with hers, behind his back. They are forced to kiss and swallow all the mixed juices together while he jams her with his ringed cock. *Now, I'm trying not to gag at this point.* He's told that she's been bad and has to tell her what a slut she is. He says things like, "Take that, you bitch." "The Mistress says you're a whore. Take that!" He'll then ask for permission to come, after which, we end the call.

Suspend Me: More discomfort, more restraints and more pain. Here we go again. Another one of his favorites is where he's put into a suspension "swing" made of leather and chains. His cock and balls are tied and bound as usual with nipple clamps already on. He's blind folded and strapped into the swing, suspended in the air and left there for a couple of hours. When the "Mistress" goes by him, his ass is slapped with a paddle, hard. On her way back, she slaps his balls until both are red and swollen.

He's temporarily brought down and put in a chair while the same black slave girl is brought in again. She has nipple clamps also and when she's put on top of him, their clamps are tied together so that they can't move without pain. Their legs are tied together as well as their arms with a leather strap around both of their necks. Then they are suspended together and left in that position for hours.

The Mistress goes by and beats both of their asses while they're hanging uncomfortably. When she decides to be entertained, he must have sex with the slave in the swing without a word until she tells him to come. She then dismisses them after they kiss her boots, say than you and back out of the room. After our conversations, he tells me about his job, home and activities. We'll carry on a "normal" conversation. I like him. He's nice.

Ice Cubes & Ice Hot: This guy is for real and is definitely my favorite of all time. He's a trip. I know he's doing everything I tell him to do and he goes on for an entire hour! Although his fetishes are odd, I enjoy talking to him. He's pleasant, always courteous and I've never had a problem with his credit card! After two years of phone calls, I've gotten to know him pretty well. He had a relationship with a woman that was full of role-play and domination as well as all the "normal" aspects. Here are some of the things she would make him do.

Come to her home, strip naked at the door and ask permission to enter, leaving his clothing outside, including shoes.

Cook for her and clean her house completely naked, with an occasional apron only. *I hope for his sake she didn't ask for bacon*!

Feed, bathe, lotion, wash, dry and comb her hair and of course, clean the bathroom afterward. Help her dress and paint her nails.

*Note: Now I understand she liked to be treated like an Egyptian princess with her own personal slave, but personally speaking, if someone did all that for me, I'd feel like an invalid!

Please her sexually, if and when she wanted it, sometimes not allowing him any sexual release at all.

Throughout their weekend, she would also "discipline" him with many, many spankings on all parts of his body and make him take numerous dildos.

Here's a typical phone call:

He calls me Mistress when I answer the phone. First order of business is telling me how he's prepared that day. He'll list the "toys" he has lined up for me, consisting of the following: A paddle, hairbrush, toothbrush, ruler, leather shoelaces, rubber bands, long cotton swabs, bowl of ice cubes, a dildo, ice/hot muscle rub, an empty cup and clothespins. *Now you see why it takes an hour?*

I'll tell him to start by putting two rubber bands around his balls, tight. Next, he takes the leather shoelaces and ties them in a figure 8 around his b's again and follows it to the base of his penis, ties it tight and puts another rubber band just under the head. I don't always have him use everything, and do change order and time. I ask him what it looks like. He'll tell me he's beginning to turn pink and swell a little. Not good enough. I want red and very swollen. He's to take the ruler, put the phone down and spank his balls for two minutes each, making sure I hear the slaps. He does it and must time it because he's always accurate.

He says "Thank you Mistress." Now he has to work on that tied up cock. He's told to lay it down on a coffee table and smack it with the paddle for two minutes, up and down the shaft, followed by two more minutes just on the head. After he catches his breath, he's told to spank the underside with the paddle for three or four minutes.

Now, let's not forget that butt. He's to suck on two ice cubes and stick them up his rear end. *The sucking is to take off any rough edges.* Then put some ice/hot muscle rub just around the butt hole. When he feels the cold start to turn hot, he's told to wet his nipples and spank them with the back of the hairbrush for two minutes each. Follow that with clothespins. Before his penis and b's stop throbbing, he's told to pee in the cup. Oh, forgot something before he gets to pee. He has to stick a cotton swab coated with the muscle rub all the way down his pee hole. OUCH! Then he can pee, after he takes out the swab. I've actually heard him nearly scream when pulling that damn thing out. *The cotton swab was entirely his doing.* I make him drink the pee. *Maybe he's really drinking apple juice. I don't know.*

After all this he'll ask if I want him to spank himself more. Sometimes I say yes, making him put the muscle rub on his balls and penis. Here's a new one and, warning, it's nasty. He has to brush his butthole with the toothbrush and paste either on the outside only or put the toothbrush inside an inch or so. Then…he has to brush his teeth. *I have to take credit for that one.*

After he's done all those things, I make him suck the dildo, call himself slutty names, use the dildo, suck it again and finally allow him to come. Well, not always. We've done some shorter calls where he's done about half of the above and is made to wear his penis and balls tied the rest of the afternoon. Then at home he must do his dildo for five minutes before coming. I've actually made him call me later in the day to report!

I'm Shocked!: I don't know about anyone else, but I really hate it when the weather is cold and you get a shock every time you get out of your car. Pisses me off! Why people want to be shocked purposely is beyond me but there are plenty who do, especially this "bad boy" client.

This guy has been bad, trying on my underwear. I catch him in my room wearing a bra, panties and stockings. He's dragged to a table and bent over with his hands tied in front of him and secured. His panties are pulled around his ankles and his balls are electrically shocked from behind. When he's faint from being shocked, he's put in a chair, hands still tied and he's belted in. His nipples and penis are shocked now and he must beg for forgiveness since he was so out of line. Imagine, not just wearing someone's underwear without permission, but wearing the Mistresses underwear! What was he thinking?

The Mistress goes between shocking him and stroking him, getting him turned on and hard and then shocking him soft again. If Mistress says it's ok, he's allowed to stroke himself with one hand only and come on the floor, which of course he has to lick up. This guy gasps for breath when I describe the shocking. It's almost like he's living it out in his mind. Oh yeah, he is.

Rubber Pants Man: From the very beginning of this one and a half phone relationship, this caller seemed odd on all levels. Not a "bad guy," just different. You'll see.

He was soft-spoken and very serious. Didn't laugh much, not a fan of comedy or anything light in nature. As a matter of fact, his favorite places to visit were third world countries. See what I mean? Most of us would choose somewhere beachy and warm, or snow capped ski lodges, but not him. He liked to be right in with the people. We're talking about places with unacceptable sanitation, water and who knows what else?

He'd call me from work, after the place was closed and would tell me what articles of clothing he had with him. I'd give him the order in which to put them on and call him back in fifteen minutes for the phone call itself. Here are the articles: A rubber glove, two pair of panties, bra, pantyhose, rubber pants, a nightie and later, a butt plug and diaper. He wanted to please the Mistress by wearing all of these at once and humiliate himself. I'd give him an order such as this: Put the rubber glove on the penis, followed by the panties, pantyhose, panties over that, the rubber pants, the nightie and then his own clothing. He'd have to go to the men's room and look into the mirror for further instructions. *The rubber glove on the penis was his idea.*

At one point he said he wanted to put an ink marker up his butt. *Don't ask. I have NO idea why.* Not a good idea, so I told him to purchase a butt plug and use that. He did, but couldn't keep it in, so I had him purchase a pair of tight, latex underpants from an adult store to hold it in for those sessions. At this point I realized that he didn't necessarily have a fetish for rubber gloves. He just liked the feel of rubber, latex and leather and was improvising.

One thing I couldn't get used to was that he'd come in the glove and save it, reusing and refilling it. Made me squeamish. He'd look in the mirror and wait for me to tell him when to take the clothing off, when to touch himself, how fast, slow, etc. That worked for a while.

He also wanted to be humiliated and do things in public. I told him to go to another town, away from his friends and family and put the clothes on, stuffing the bra with cum filled gloves and letting the strap show through his dress shirt. He was to go to a convenience store and buy condoms. He obeyed, supposedly. .

One time I had him go through a fast food drive-through and pee himself as he was paying at the window. I told him it would be so embarrassing if he had to stop and get out of the car for any reason. *A friend gave me this idea. OK, so I have strange friends.*

Another time, I told him to wear a diaper and go into three separate stores. He had to wear the bra too and make sure that when he walked, his diaper would make noise so that everyone would know he was wearing one.

He eventually stopped calling because his significant other found the bills and he confessed to calling a sex line. I wonder if he told her what he talked about or what he did? Nah…I doubt it.

Smother Me With That Fat Ass: This particular client, in his thirties, likes to be smothered, and dominated. So, I thought I'd try something interesting with him.

He'd be my sex slave but wasn't doing things right. He didn't please me well and would have to be punished. He'd be tied naked, hands and feet to the bed, anticipating what his mistress, me, would do. Mistress enters the room, wearing a long, red gown, low cut with a high slit, revealing thigh high boots and who knows what underneath. He's not allowed to see. The Mistress approaches her slave who is helpless and expecting a whipping. No, she has no whip or paddle with her. He is scolded for not pleasing properly and must prove worthy of the Mistress again. He agrees to do anything to become accepted.

A door is opened and an extremely large woman enters. She is very heavy and is wearing a black, see through, baby doll top and bottom. I instruct her to take the bottoms off. She does. She is ordered to climb up and straddle this bad slave over his chest. Because of her weight she can't hold herself up and falls on top of him. He sighs. I tell him that it's going to get better. She is very hard to please and if he is to prove himself worthy of the Mistress, he must lick her until she comes.

With that, she climbs on his face and grinds herself against him. I see that this large woman is smothering him and I tell her to move back for exactly ten seconds. Just long enough for him to catch his breath. The timer is on and when it's over, she gets back on his face and starts again.

Over and over I let her smother his face with her big rear end and belly, giving him just enough time in between rounds not to suffocate. He is smothered for a while until Mistress feels he's had enough. The large woman in the baby doll is allowed to get down and stroke him until he comes.

This guy was totally into this fantasy and the next time he called I had the same big lady smother him with her gigantic boobs!

*Note: No disrespect intended for the large ladies out there. I'm relating a story and these were his requests. He really prefers larger women. It's the smothering part that landed in him in this section.

You're Not Worthy: "So, you think you're worthy to serve this Mistress? I don't think you're worthy to touch the Mistress or even think about it. Let's see how you can prove yourself." That's how this call started. He gave me an idea of what he'd like in advance and when he called, that's how our conversation began. He got right into it. This guy had a shoe/foot fetish with a domination twist.

"Oh yes Mistress. I'll prove myself to you." "We'll see. Take your clothes off, you worthless slave and kneel before me." "Yes Maam." He replied. "Now, give me your hands." They would be tied tightly behind his back. Now, naked, on his knees, the toe of a shiny boot is put before his mouth. "Lick it, you good for nothing slave!" He makes licking sounds over the phone. "That's not good enough. I didn't think you were worth it." "Please Mistress…." he begs, "give me another chance."

After a moment of silence, with the toe of the boot under his chin, he is told to suck the heel. "Yes Mistress." Now there are sucking sounds over the phone. "Suck it like it was a cock. Take all of this spiked cock down your throat, you slut!" More sucking sounds. "That's better."

The Mistress sits in her red velvet chair and without warning pushes the slave to the ground with both feet on his shoulders. With his hands still tied, he cannot get up easily, nor is he allowed to. He is to lay there and suck one heel while the other is pushed onto his chest. He must repeat, "I'm only worthy to suck your heels and lick your boots clean. Please let me suck your heels." *I can only imagine what the phone receiver looked like by now!* He did a pretty good job and was told he'd be allowed to do it again. If and when he becomes worthy, he can lick my toes.

Things I've Made "Submissives" Do:

Some crazy things I've told them to do on and off the phone. For the record, I think more than half did them.

*Wear ladies panties and/or pantyhose to work. This may not sound too strong but think about it. Imagine a guy wearing pink thongs on a construction job in the summer. Lots of looks when he bends over! Or, the guy at the office who can't explain the static electricity because his dress slacks are sticking to his pantyhose! Mom always said to wear clean underwear in case of an emergency. What a kick it would be they were satin and lace bikinis.

*Wear a diaper to work. Not much to explain on this one. The sound when the guy sat down would be enough.

*Wear a butt plug and walk around the mall.

*Go to a lingerie store and ask the saleslady to be fitted for a bra.

*Try one on, buy it. Make sure she knows it's not for anyone else.

*Sit in a bowl of cool gelatin with balls submerged. Stay there until it cools enough to make an impression. *Shows patience…or insanity.*

*Wear a weight on balls and stand in a hallway with legs apart for twenty minutes. *Hurts, but proves loyalty.*

*Take markers and write "Sissy boy" all over the body. Take a picture and send it to the Mistress.

*Shave a designated name or word in chest hair.

*Shave all pubic hair and/or shave legs.

*Summertime. Shave armpits and wear tank tops in public.

Use bright colored hair dye all over body hair like blue and pink.

*Write "I am your slave" five hundred times and mail it to me.

*Tie up b's with leather laces, wear panties, pantyhose plus a bra and go to a public place, like a large office building. Take a pocket tape recorder and record yourself as you're walking around, saying how turned on you are wearing all those items. Imagine overhearing that one, thinking it was some guy dictating something for his secretary?

*I love this one......Stick three ice cubes up the butt and go out for a walk. What a drag that would be, or should I say, what a drip?

Public Humiliation:

This goes along with the domination fetishes but to be more specific. These are people who actually enjoy being humiliated in public. Not just yelled at or scolded, but made fun of and ridiculed. Speaking only for myself, I certainly don't have the temperament to handle that one!

Slap Me In Public: A man with a public humiliation fantasy called and asked me to describe how I'd start a fight with him in public and call him names.

I told him we'd get dressed and go to a classy restaurant. He'd be wearing a nice sport coat, dress slacks, dress shirt and tie and I'd be in a sexy cocktail dress, expensive shoes and purse. We'd have an elegant meal and toward the end I'd start an argument with him. I'd get a little loud and say, "You did what? You slept with that slut while we were still together?" He'd try to keep me calm which would work just long enough for the people who heard it to go back to their dinners. I'd say loudly, "You screwed her sister too, didn't you!" He'd start apologizing but I'd get up from the table and tell him he's a disgusting pig. I'd throw the glass of ice water at him and tell him that maybe that would cool off his hot pants. I'd get up, grab my purse and storm toward the door. He'd immediately follow, pleading for me to come back.

On the way out, I'd turn to him and say, "It's not like you're any good anyway. It only lasts a minute!" He runs out of the restaurant to follow me, but hasn't paid the bill yet, so the staff follows us to the parking lot where I continue fighting with him, giving him a slap in the face in front of everyone. I get in the car and he tries to follow but the manger of the restaurant tells him he needs to pay the bill. I take off in a cloud of smoke in his expensive car and leave him there.

As a movie scene, maybe, but as a sexual turn on? I don't get it.

At The Bar: This guy said he wanted to be made fun of sexually and publicly. I suggested that we'd be in a bar together for a happy hour. Somewhere around dinner time when the people are still coherent. There would be a group of ladies there that I work with and I introduce them to this man as someone I've been seeing. We all enjoy a couple of drinks and the conversation turns to sex.

One of the girls asks me how the sex is with this guy. I laugh and tell her that it's lousy because he has a very small penis and can't stay hard. One of the other girls hears and before long there are five of us all talking about his small, inadequate penis. Everyone is looking at this guy. I turn to him and tell him what we're talking about, out loud, in front of everyone, including the female bartender. He says he's embarrassed and feels humiliated. I just laugh at him and so does everyone else. I tell the girls to "watch this" and take my hand to his pants. I hold up my little finger and say, "That's all he has girls. Anyone want some?" Everyone yells, "No thanks." I tell him he's good for nothing in bed and that he might as well go jerk off in the men's room. He should do it now.

He goes to the men's room while the six of us huddle by the door to listen. Of course, we all say things to him like, "Are you using both fingers?" and "Can you find it?" This turns him on even more and we all applaud when he comes.

Note: I wonder if in real life, this really is the guy with the ten inches!

I've Been Such A Jerk!: This particular man said he wanted to be publicly scolded for doing something wrong. OK....let me think. Got it. I told him that he stood me up for a date on my birthday and that I'd never go out with him again. He calls my office and apologizes but I tell him it's not good enough. So, I put in on speakerphone for the entire office staff to hear. I tell him to apologize to me in front of everyone. He says he's sorry which makes them all snicker. I tell him it wasn't loud enough and to beg me to forgive him. He does. I tell him to pretend to cry. He does. Now the staff is outright laughing! I take him off speakerphone and say something privately. After an hour I ask everyone in the office to go to the window.

There he is, outside in the parking lot with a big sign covering himself, wearing only a pair of boxers with hearts all over them. The sign says, "I'm sorry. I've been a jerk!". Everyone opens the windows and yells things at him. "You're a jerk all right!" "You're nuts too!" "Forgot your pants?" To make it worse and to end his fantasy, I tell him to go away, slam the window and watch as a police cruiser pulls up and takes him away. He thought this was great.

CONCLUSION

There are so many more stories in each category, and so many we haven't even touched on that I could write another book. *Hey, not a bad idea!* I hope for now I gave you enough to entertain you. I also hope that I've helped you to understand the many different aspects of this business.... That although there are some weirdoes and freaks, most are just regular people trying to express themselves. Remember that there are weirdoes and freaks in all sorts of businesses. I hope you see that both strippers and phone sex people are just that, people, with feelings, goals and lives, as well as the clients who call and visit them. There are good and bad in all. Hopefully we can all focus on the good.

Thank you for joining me on this adventure and I hope you had fun!

ABOUT THE AUTHOR:

Maria DeStefano, a native Bostonian who became an exotic dancer at the unusual age of forty and started a phone sex line at forty six. With curiosities from both men and women, she combined a flare for writing and entertaining, bringing these fun-filled, true stories to you. Contact her at MariaD127@Yahoo.com.

Book Description

Enter the world of the Adult Entertainment Industry. Have you ever wondered what it's like to be an exotic dancer? What are the girls really like, what happens at the clubs and who visits them? How about bachelor parties? Or…how about those phone sex lines? Who calls and what does the lady behind the phone truly look like?

Come with me on an adventure, from night club dressing rooms, to the stage, to the thoughts of clients. Meet the girls and hear personal stories. Then we'll journey into the private world of phone sex. Hear revealing conversations, fantasies, fetishes and more.

This book promises to enlighten and entertain with a humorous view of this industry and a bit of the serious side thrown in. Be warned though…once you start reading, you might not want to stop. Definite adult material.

0-595-24420-3

www.ingramcontent.com/pod-product-compliance
Lightning Source LLC
Chambersburg PA
CBHW061400280526
45784CB00001B/316